CONTEMPORA

CITIZENSHIP NOW

A GUIDE FOR NATURALIZATION

ALIZA BECKER AND LAURIE EDWARDS
IN COOPERATION WITH
TRAVELERS AND IMMIGRANTS AID OF CHICAGO

CB

CONTEMPORARY BOOKS

a division of NTC/CONTEMPORARY PUBLISHING COMPANY
Lincolnwood, Illinois USA

Library of Congress Cataloging-in-Publication Data
Becker, Aliza, 1958–
        Contemporary's citizenship now: a guide for naturalization/
Aliza Becker and Laurie Edwards.
        p.   cm.
        1. Citizenship—United States—Popular works. 2. Naturalization
–United States—Handbooks, manuals, etc. 3. United States—Politics
and government—Popular works. 4. United States—History—Popular
works. 5. Civics—Popular works. 6. English language—Textbooks
for foreign speakers.   I. Edwards, Laurie.   II. Title.
JK1758.B54   1995
323.6'0973—dc20   95-24850
                                                            CIP

Photo Credits
Cover   Statue of Liberty, FPG International/ © Richard Laird, 1993; Liberty Bell, FPG
International/ © Steven Gottlieb, 1992
Interior   Pages 1, 7, 17, 37, 49, 52, 89, 98/Michael A. Schwarz, 1995; Pages 2, 13, 18,
31, 43, 45, 47, 53, 55, 63a, 63b, 63d, 70, 83, 84, 95, 109, 113/Tribune File Photos;
Pages 22, 136/Stock Montage; Pages 27, 69, 79/Arturo Lopez; Pages 41, 42, 63c, 73,
91, 100, 101, 103/Bettmann Archive; Page 108/Thomas Scharf

Project Editor
Christine Kelner

ISBN: 0-8092-3270-7

Published by Contemporary Books,
a division of NTC/Contemporary Publishing Company,
4255 West Touhy Avenue,
Lincolnwood (Chicago), Illinois 60646-1975 U.S.A.
© 1990 by NTC/Contemporary Publishing Company
All rights reserved. No part of this book may be reproduced,
stored in a retrieval system, or transmitted in any form or by any means,
electronic, mechanical, photocopying, recording, or otherwise,
without prior permission of the publisher.
Manufactured in the United States of America.

7 8 9 0 GB 11 10 9 8 7 6

Director, New Product Development Noreen Lopez *Editorial Director* Mark Boone	*Editorial* Alan Kimmel Sharon Rundo Bernice Rappoport Edward Roberts	*Design and Production Manager* Norma Underwood *Cover and Interior Design* Michael Kelly	*Production Artist* Thomas D. Scharf *Electronic Composition* Victoria A. Randall

TABLE OF CONTENTS

ACKNOWLEDGMENTS

The authors would like to thank Suzanne Leibman for bringing them together for this project. They would also like to thank their colleagues and families for giving them time, space, and technical support.

In addition, the authors acknowledge the following individuals for their help in reviewing the manuscript for *Citizenship Now*:

Peggy Dean, Resource Consultant, Adult Learning Resource Center, Adult Education Service Center of Northern Illinois

Jennifer De Leon, Citizenship Education Facilitator, Chicago Community Link, Travelers & Immigrants Aid of Chicago

Bernadine Karge, attorney, Midwest Immigrant Rights Center, Travelers & Immigrants Aid of Chicago

Marketa Lindt, attorney, Citizenship and Immigration Coordinator, Illinois Coalition for Immigrant and Refugee Protection

Roy Petty, attorney, Senior Director, Midwest Immigrant Rights Center, Travelers & Immigrants Aid of Chicago

Linda Traeger, Chief Operating Officer, Travelers & Immigrants Aid of Chicago

The research involved in developing the manuscript for this text is based in part on material from *Building Bridges: A Resource Guide on Citizenship* by Aliza Becker, Curriculum Publications Clearinghouse at Western Illinois University © 1993 by the Illinois State Board of Education. The project to develop these materials was awarded to Travelers & Immigrants Aid by the Illinois State Board of Education, Adult Education & Literacy Section, with funding from the U.S. Department of Education, Section 353 Demonstration Projects.

Contemporary Books wishes to express its gratitude to Adriana Sanchez-Aldana of the Adult Resource Center, Chula Vista, California, for her assistance in determining the contents of *Citizenship Now*, for her review of and recommendations for an early chapter of the book, and for her willing participation throughout this project in providing information and resources necessary for its completion.

Contemporary Books also wishes to thank William Gonzales, Instituto del Progreso Latino, Chicago, Illinois, and Paul Metzger, Houston Community College, Citizenship Center, Houston, Texas, for their initial direction and advice on the preparation of materials for *Citizenship Now*.

Finally, Contemporary Books gratefully acknowledges the cooperation and interest of staff from CASAS and ETS, who provided samples of their respective tests, answer sheets, and test procedures for duplication in *Citizenship Now*. The prompt responses from CASAS and ETS staff to inquiries is equally appreciated.

Citizenship Now: A Guide for Naturalization is an English as a Second Language citizenship preparation textbook for high-beginning/low-intermediate students. It is designed for use:

    a. by students applying to become naturalized U.S. citizens, and

    b. in a classroom setting or for self study.

Through speaking, listening, reading, and writing, it specifically teaches the information and skills necessary to:

    a. complete the Application for Naturalization (N-400),

    b. be successful in the Immigration and Naturalization Service (INS) naturalization interview, and

    c. pass the U.S. history and government and English literacy tests required for naturalization.

The book can be used either as a core textbook for citizenship classes or as a supplemental text in other classes. The book invites students to acquire knowledge about their adopted country by building on their unique cultures and heritages. It also encourages active citizenry through public participation.

The Naturalization Process

Naturalization is the legal process by which people with lawful permanent resident status (LPR) can obtain U.S. citizenship. To become naturalized citizens, applicants must fulfill certain requirements, which include proving they are legally eligible and, for most people, passing both an English literacy and a U.S. history and government test.

Applicants must demonstrate basic English reading, writing, listening, and speaking skills. Listening and speaking are tested at the INS interview. The interviewer wants to see that the applicant can follow simple instructions and respond to basic questions related to the N-400. An applicant can meet the reading and writing requirement by passing a standardized citizenship test prior to the interview or at the interview itself. An applicant who takes the test at the interview is asked to write one or more dictated sentences and may be asked to read from a book or form.

Applicants can fulfill the U.S. history and government requirement by taking a standardized test prior to the interview or at the interview itself. Sometimes applicants take a multiple-choice test at the interview to expedite large numbers of applicants, although answering oral questions based on the INS List of 100 Questions on U.S. History and Government for the Naturalization Interview (September 1994 update) is more the norm. According to immigration regulations, the interviewer should adjust the difficulty of the questions asked to the background of the applicant.

The requirements for naturalization described in this book are current to the date of publication, but they are subject to change. The INS is considering several substantive changes to expedite the naturalization process. It is important that instructors be aware of any procedural changes that they must pass on to their students.

The current process involves the following steps:

(a) An immigrant meets the eligibility requirements for naturalization.

(b) She or he submits the N-400, fingerprints, photos, photocopy of the Resident Alien Card, and money order to the INS.

(c) A standardized citizenship test may be taken. (If this is the case, the N-400 must be filed within a year of taking the test.)

(d) The applicant goes to an INS interview. Oral English skills are tested at the interview. (If not done in step *c*, history and government and written English skills are tested at the interview as well.)

(e) The new citizen takes an oath of allegiance at a swearing-in ceremony.

The Format

This textbook includes essential information for persons wishing to pass the INS English and history and government tests for naturalization. Additional contextual information has been included to make the content more meaningful and to provide knowledge that empowers new citizens to productively contribute to their community and country.

In every chapter, low-level readings are preceded by questions and visuals that set the stage for that particular topic. Although the first chapter deals with the process of naturalization, subsequent chapters present the information necessary to pass the U.S. history and government test. The final chapters focus on voting and public participation as a citizen and include a review of the essential information covered in the book. You will note that in the readings, the first sentence of each paragraph is bolded to highlight the main idea.

The readings are followed by multiple-choice test questions* to which students are asked to respond on standardized test answer sheets. These questions are designed to replicate as closely as possible the actual questions and format of standardized U.S. citizenship tests. Teachers are encouraged to follow actual testing procedures provided in the appendix to give students a chance to become familiar with the test setting. Since test questions may be presented orally in the actual testing situation, many of these multiple-choice questions are included also on the audiocasette designed to accompany the text.

Vocabulary words for the readings, presented in list format, are reinforced by a variety of exercises that come after the readings. These exercises combine vocabulary in context with open-ended discussion questions to personalize the material for all learners. These exercises are designed to develop and strengthen language skills that will help students successfully complete the test requirements.

* This section includes essential information needed to pass the standardized citizenship tests.

Each chapter focuses on a portion of the N-400. Sections included from the actual form allow students to formulate answers on paper. Students may then practice the possible interview questions provided that relate to that portion of the application. Although vocabulary from the N-400 is used in context, additional practice on these words and phrases may be necessary for some students.

Practice on such functional interview skills as asking for clarification and reporting personal information is included throughout the book. Because answering questions orally is the current measure of oral proficiency in English, the interview dialogues in each chapter are designed to help students prepare for the kinds of questions they may be asked in their INS interview. Interview questions are also included on the audiocasette so that students can practice answering oral questions using information about themselves.

Dictation practice* and questions from the INS List of 100 Questions on U.S. History and Government for the Naturalization Interview (September, 1994)* included in *Citizenship Now* enable students to practice for these portions of the naturalization process as well. Teachers are encouraged to use the audiotaped versions of these exercises to give students a chance to listen to speakers with various accents and voices.

Finally, each chapter contains a short English grammar lesson. Each grammar point was chosen to give students practice with language skills necessary for the naturalization interview. Each lesson also reviews U.S. history and government facts.

The Appendix includes sample standardized tests, testing procedures, and all items on the INS List of 100 Questions on U.S. History and Government for the Naturalization Interview. A student who can pass these tests and answer these questions, as well as those from the sample INS interview in the final chapter, should be adequately prepared to meet the English and history and government naturalization requirements.

The Role of the Citizenship Preparation Instructor

Instructors should be cautioned against giving specific legal advice or helping students to fill out their actual N-400 forms (**Application for Naturalization**). The instructor is *not* qualified to discuss the implications of this information or to offer opinions on particular cases. Immigration regulations provide that only four groups of people can provide legal representation before the INS: (1) lawyers, (2) Board of Immigration Appeals (BIA) Accredited Representatives, (3) law school graduates and supervised law students, and (4) reputable individuals who help a friend or family member.

* This section includes essential information needed to pass the standardized and oral citizenship tests.

Although students may meet with legal providers to fill out their applications, the instructor is the person with whom they will have the most consistent contact. Therefore, the instructor is the one to whom students will bring many of their questions. Remembering that naturalization is a legal process, the instructor can refer students to agencies that offer legal advice and to reputable lawyers or hotlines that answer legal questions by phone. The instructor can also supply definitions, official dates, costs, locations, and other general information.

Naturalization is a fairly routine process for most people; however, certain people should NOT apply for citizenship. These persons may not only be rejected, but they also may endanger their LPR (Lawful Permanent Resident) status. In a worst case scenario, they may be deported and prohibited from reentering the United States. The instructor can provide an additional layer of screening by referring for legal consultation anyone with criminal convictions, possible marriage or welfare fraud, or lengthy absences from the United States as a permanent resident.

None of this diminishes the significant role that citizenship preparation instructors play in preparing their students to pass both the English and the U.S. history and government tests. Many applicants view these tests as a huge obstacle to overcome. Some have not taken a test for many years, and others may have never taken a standardized test. Instructors can be instrumental in building students' confidence and self-esteem.

In addition, some students feel a great deal of pressure to get their citizenship; often, family members' immigration to the United States depends on the student obtaining his or her citizenship. It is therefore important that students believe in themselves and in their ability to make it through the process successfully.

Citizenship classes are also an ideal forum for students to look at public participation in the institutions of our democratic system. The right to vote is one of the most important tools of our democracy. It is available to those who successfully naturalize. During class, students can discuss ways to participate fully in their community and country and thus learn how our national institutions can help them lead meaningful, productive lives.

* * * * * * *

This book is dedicated to all immigrants, past and future, whose presence here has made this country great.

Citizenship Now was written in collaboration with the *La Place* Program for Educational Opportunity.

CHAPTER 1

Steps to Citizenship

New U.S. citizens come from all over the world.

Getting into the Reading

1. Where are the people in the picture above?

2. How do you think they are feeling?

3. What are they doing?

4. Why do people want to become U.S. citizens?

5. When will you apply to become a U.S. citizen?

6. Why do you want to become a U.S. citizen?

7. How will you feel when you become a U.S. citizen?

Words to Know

amnesty	naturalization	standardized test
deported	naturalized	swearing-in ceremony
eligible	oath of allegiance	symbol
fingerprints	permanent resident	truth
INS interview	petition	

Why Become a U.S. Citizen?

There are many benefits to becoming a U.S. citizen. Every year many people become naturalized, or are given rights, as U.S. citizens.

The most important benefit is the right to vote in elections. Your vote is very important to the democratic process. You can vote for someone who represents your opinions. In this way, you can play a part in the U.S. government.

If you are a citizen, you can file a petition (the I-130 form) to legally bring your parents, unmarried children who are minors, and husband or wife to the United States. Generally, they will get their permanent resident (or legal) status quickly. Citizens can also bring their adult children (single or married) and brothers and sisters here, although getting permanent residence for them will take longer. As a permanent resident, however, you can petition, or request, to bring only a wife, husband, or unmarried children of any age, although these family members cannot immigrate right away.

As a U.S. citizen, you can travel for a long time outside of the United States with your passport. You can also live outside of the United States. As a permanent resident, however, you may lose your legal residence status and not be allowed to return if you leave the United States for more than six months at a time.

A U.S. citizen <u>cannot</u> be deported, or sent back to his or her native country, but a permanent resident <u>can</u> be deported and may not be allowed to return. U.S. citizenship is protection against deportation.

How to Become a U.S. Citizen

Naturalization is the process by which persons who were not born in the United States become U.S. citizens. You may be eligible, or qualified, for naturalization if you have been a permanent resident for five years or if you have been married to a U.S. citizen for three years. You can apply for citizenship three months before you are eligible.

First, you must fill out the Application for Naturalization (the N-400). You must tell the truth on the N-400. If you do not tell the truth, or if you make a mistake, the Immigration and Naturalization Service (INS) may ask you difficult questions.

You can take the application to the INS office with pictures of yourself, your fingerprints, a money order, and a copy of your Resident Alien Card (green card). Then, you will receive a date for your INS interview.

At the INS interview, the INS examiner will ask you questions in English about your application and documents. This is done to test your English-speaking skills. If you do not understand a question, you can ask the examiner to repeat the question or say it in different words.

Some people take a test at the INS interview. At the interview, the INS examiner will ask you questions in English about U.S. history and government. The INS examiner will also ask you to read something in English and to write down something he or she says to you in English.

Some people do not have to take a test at the INS interview. You will not be tested if you:

(1) passed a standardized citizenship test before the interview (and give the INS examiner your test results) or

(2) passed the English and U.S. history and government test during the amnesty program of the late 1980s.

There are other people who do not have to take either the English speaking test or the U.S. history and government test. See the Appendix for more information about this.

After the INS interview, you will receive a letter from the INS with a date for the swearing-in ceremony. Usually, a judge will have you take an oath of allegiance, or a promise to be faithful to the United States, and give you a naturalization certificate. After the ceremony, you can register to vote, obtain a U.S. passport, and petition to bring your family to the United States. You will have the full rights of U.S. citizenship.

The Statue of Liberty

The Statue of Liberty is a symbol of freedom and international friendship. It was given to the United States by France in 1884.

Because of its location in New York City's harbor, the Statue of Liberty is the first thing many immigrants to the United States see when they arrive in this country. Each year about two million people visit the Statue of Liberty.

Getting Information from the Reading

 A. Choose the best answer for each of these questions. Fill in the correct circle on the answer sheet to the right. The first one is done for you.

1. Which answer below is a benefit of U.S. citizenship?

   a. You can vote in elections.
   b. You can petition to bring some of your family to the United States.
   c. You cannot be deported.
   d. all of the above

2. If you are a U.S. citizen and have a passport, you can travel to Chile and return to the United States

   a. after six months.
   b. after nine months.
   c. after three years.
   d. all of the above

3. To apply for U.S. citizenship, most people must be permanent residents for

   a. one year.
   b. five years.
   c. ten years.
   d. fifteen years.

4. What is the citizenship application called?

   a. I-130
   b. N-400
   c. W-2
   d. I-698

5. What is the Statue of Liberty a symbol of?

   a. freedom
   b. citizenship
   c. travel
   d. love

6. What will you do at the swearing-in ceremony?

   a. take an oath of allegiance
   b. take an English test
   c. fill out the N-400
   d. none of the above

Answer Sheet

1. ⓐ ⓑ ⓒ ●

2. ⓐ ⓑ ⓒ ⓓ

3. ⓐ ⓑ ⓒ ⓓ

4. ⓐ ⓑ ⓒ ⓓ

5. ⓐ ⓑ ⓒ ⓓ

6. ⓐ ⓑ ⓒ ⓓ

Test Tip

On a multiple-choice test, you sometimes know that at least one of the possible answers is wrong. Look among the rest of the possible answers for the correct one. Which answer looks correct? If you are not sure, GUESS.

B. Write the correct word or words in each blank to complete the sentences below. Use the words listed in the box on page 1. You may not use all of the words in the box. The first one is done for you.

1. U.S. citizens can file a _____*petition*_____ to bring their parents to the United States.

2. Polish citizens can become U.S. citizens by the process of _____ _____.

3. You may be eligible for citizenship if you have lived in the United States for five years as a _____.

4. Permanent residents can be sent back, or _____, to their native country if they commit certain crimes or leave the United States for a long time.

5. On your N-400, you must tell the _____.

6. At the _____, people must be ready to answer questions in English about their application.

7. To become a citizen, you must take an oath of _____.

8. At the _____ you will become a U.S. citizen.

C. Answer these questions orally. Use short answers.

1. Why do you want to become a U.S. citizen? Which benefits are most important for you?

2. When will you be eligible to become a U.S. citizen?

3. Have you taken any steps to become a U.S. citizen? Which ones?

4. What worries you about the interview? Your ability to speak English? Your ability to understand the interviewer? The dictation? Remembering your U.S. history and government facts? Reading English? How will you prepare?

5. As a new citizen, what is the first thing you will do?

The N-400 Application: Parts 1, 2, and 3

Below are parts 1, 2, and 3 of the Application for Naturalization (N-400). Write information about yourself in the blanks.

U.S. Department of Justice
Immigration and Naturalization Service

START HERE - Please Type or Print

Part 1. Information about you.

Family Name	Given Name	Middle Initial

U.S. Mailing Address - Care of

Street Number and Name		Apt. #
City	County	
State	ZIP Code	

Date of Birth (month/day/year)	Country of Birth
Social Security #	A #

Part 2. Basis for Eligibility (check one).

a. ☐ I have been a permanent resident for at least five (5) years.

b. ☐ I have been a permanent resident for at least three (3) years and have been married to a United States Citizen for those three years.

c. ☐ I am a permanent resident child of United States citizen parent(s).

d. ☐ I am applying on the basis of qualifying military service in the Armed Forces of the U.S. and have attached completed Forms N-426 and G-325B

e. ☐ Other. (Please specify section of law) _____

Part 3. Additional information about you.

Date you became a permanent resident (month/day/year)	Port admitted with an immmigrant visa or INS Office where granted adjustment of status.
Citizenship	

Name on alien registration card (if different than in Part 1)

Other names used since you became a permanent resident (including maiden name)

Sex	☐ Male ☐ Female	Height	Marital Status:	☐ Single ☐ Married	☐ Divorced ☐ Widowed

Can you speak, read and write English ? ☐No ☐Yes.

Absences from the U.S.:

Have you been absent from the U.S. since becoming a permanent resident? ☐ No ☐Yes.

If you answered "Yes", complete the following, Begin with your most recent absence. If you need more room to explain the reason for an absence or to list more trips, continue on separate paper.

Date left U.S.	Date returned	Did absence last 6 months or more?	Destination	Reason for trip
		☐ Yes ☐ No		
		☐ Yes ☐ No		
		☐ Yes ☐ No		
		☐ Yes ☐ No		
		☐ Yes ☐ No		
		☐ Yes ☐ No		

Form N-400 (Rev. 07/17/91)N   *Continued on back.*

TEN BASIC CITIZENSHIP REQUIREMENTS

1. You are a permanent resident now, and you have been a permanent resident for five years.*

2. You are 18 years or older OR you will be 18 at the time of your INS interview.

3. You have made a home in the United States for at least five years AND you have lived in your state for at least three months.*

4. You have lived in the United States for at least 2 1/2 years (50 percent) of the 5-year period.*

5. You have not abandoned, or given up, your residence or left the United States for a long period of time.

6. You can speak and understand English at the INS interview.

7. You can pass an English reading and writing test.

8. You can pass a test on basic U.S. history and government.

9. You have good moral character.

10. You will take an oath of allegiance.

*You can apply for U.S. citizenship after three (3) years if you have been a permanent resident for three (3) years and have been married to a U.S. citizen for those three years.

(See the Appendix for a more complete explanation of citizenship requirements, including exceptions to the requirements.)

THE INS INTERVIEW

A. Practice this dialogue with a partner.

INS: Let me check some information. What is your complete name?
You: My name is Maria Elena Morales.

INS: What is your home address?
You: My address is 6724 Main Street, Apartment 5, Waukegan, Illinois. The zip code is 62085.

INS: May I please have your passport, Resident Alien Card, and a photo ID? Your driver's license or state ID is fine.
You: I'm sorry. I don't understand your question.
INS: I need your passport, your green card, and a photo ID.
You: Oh, sure. Here you are.

INS: Your current citizenship is?
You: Sorry?
INS: What is your citizenship now?
You: I am a Mexican citizen.
INS: What was your port of entry?
You: Laredo, Texas.
INS: What is your marital status?
You: I am married.
INS: Have you been married before?
You: Do you mean, was I married before I came to the United States?
INS: No. Were you ever married to anyone else?
You: Oh. No.
INS: Have you left the United States since you became a permanent resident?
You: Yes. I went back to Mexico one time.
INS: For how long?
You: I was there for three weeks to visit my family.

B. Now practice the dialogue using correct information about yourself.

C. During the INS interview, the interviewer will read a sentence to you. You then must write the sentence correctly in English. Practice by listening carefully and writing the sentences that you hear. The first one is done for you.

1. *I live in the United States of America.*

2. _____

3. _____

4. _____

5. _____

The Standardized Citizenship Test

What is a standardized citizenship test?

It is a multiple-choice test, approved by the INS, that you can take at a testing place in your community before your INS naturalization interview. The Educational Testing Service (ETS) and the Comprehensive Adult Student Assessment System (CASAS) are two of the biggest companies that give this test. The questions on pages four and eight of this chapter are similar to the ones found on these tests. There are questions like these in every chapter of this book.

What are the advantages in taking a standardized citizenship test?

(1) If you pass this test before your naturalization interview, you will not be asked any U.S. history or government questions during your interview. Your English reading and writing skills will not be tested at the interview either.

(2) You can take this test as many times as you need to. If you do not pass it, you can take the test again.

(3) You have to get only 12 out of the 20 multiple-choice questions correct and write down correctly one or two sentences that you hear.

What are the disadvantages in taking a standardized citizenship test?

(1) There is a fee for taking the test.

(2) The test results are good for only one year. You have to apply for naturalization before the end of that year.

GETTING TO KNOW ENGLISH

Information Questions

- What?
- Why?

- How?
- When?

- Where?
- Who?

Many questions in English start with the words above. These questions ask for information. You cannot answer these questions by saying just "yes" or "no."

 A. Match each question word with a correct answer by drawing a line between them. The first one is done for you.

1. Where?
2. When?
3. How?
4. Why?
5. Who?
6. What?

a. My brother
b. Last year
c. Because I want to become a citizen
d. In Japan
e. My green card
f. My name is spelled L-E-E

 B. Practice answering some questions starting with these words.

1. What is your complete name?
2. How do you spell your family name?
3. Why do you want to become a U.S. citizen?
4. When did you become a permanent resident?
5. Where were you born?
6. Who is your husband/wife?

✎ **C. Now write the correct question word in each blank. The first one is done for you.**

Who　　　*What*　　　*When*　　　*Where*　　　*How*　　　*Why*

1. ___*What*___ is your address? (My address is 435 W. Oak Street.)

2. _____ were you born? (I was born on October 3, 1976.)

3. _____ were you born? (I was born in São Paulo, Brazil.)

4. _____ did you come to the United States? (because my brother lives here)

5. _____ did you come to the United States? (in 1992)

6. _____ did you go back to China? (to visit my parents)

7. _____ did you go back to China? (in 1993)

8. _____ did you go back to China? (by plane)

9. _____ do you live with? (my children and parents)

10. _____ date did you become a permanent resident? (July 7, 1989)

11. _____ did you become a permanent resident? (July 7, 1989)

12. _____ did you become a permanent resident? (because I want to become a citizen some day)

13. _____ did you become a permanent resident? (in New York City)

14. _____ did you become a permanent resident? (through the amnesty program)

CHAPTER 2

The New World

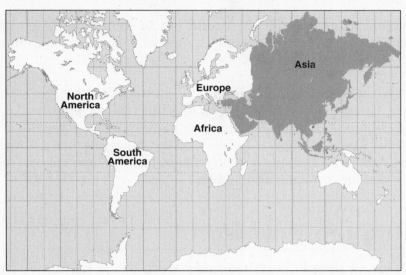

At the time of Columbus, Europeans made long and difficult trips to Asia for goods and spices.

Getting into the Reading

1. What did you learn about Christopher Columbus in your native country?

2. Can you find your native country and the following countries, seas, oceans, or states on a world map?

Atlantic Ocean	Spain	New Mexico
United States	India	Mexico
Caribbean Sea	England	Virginia
Massachusetts		

3. Why did people want to travel to the New World?

4. How did they travel to the New World?

5. Why did you want to come to the United States?

Words to Know

colonist	discover	practice	settle	tobacco
colony	form	reach	silk	trade
crops	native	sailors	spices	

Discovering the New World

Christopher Columbus wanted to go to Asia to find gold, silk, and spices, but it took a long time to travel from Europe to Asia by land. Europeans wanted to find a shorter way to get there.

Christopher Columbus thought he could get to Asia by sailing westward across the Atlantic Ocean. The queen of Spain gave Columbus sailors and three ships to sail to Asia.

On October 12, 1492, Columbus *reached* some islands in the Caribbean Sea. Columbus thought he was in India, so he called the people who lived there Indians. Later, people realized that Columbus had come to a place the Europeans did not know. We now call this land the Americas. We call the people who lived there American Indians or Native Americans. Christopher Columbus discovered America for the Spanish in 1492.

Colonizing the New World

Around 1600, many people began coming from other countries to live in what is now the United States. The people lived in colonies. A colony is an area under the control of a distant country and is often settled by people from that country.

Colonists from Spain and Mexico settled in what is now New Mexico in the southwestern part of the United States in 1598. This was a Spanish colony and then a part of Mexico. Later it became part of the United States.

The first permanent English colony was founded in 1607 at Jamestown, Virginia. The English colonists grew tobacco to trade with England.

In 1620, the Pilgrims traveled to America on a ship called the *Mayflower*. They were not free to practice their religion in Europe. The Pilgrims wanted religious freedom, so they came to North America. They formed the colony of Plymouth in the state we now call Massachusetts.

The first year at Plymouth was very difficult for the Pilgrims. They were sick and hungry. Many died. Native Americans helped the Pilgrims to plant crops, to hunt, and to fish.

In 1621, the Pilgrims had plenty of food to eat. They had a big celebration to give thanks. They invited the Native Americans to their celebration.

Today this celebration is known as the holiday of Thanksgiving. It takes place on the fourth Thursday in November. Many people eat turkey, sweet potatoes, corn, and cranberries to remember the food at the first Thanksgiving. This is a special family holiday of thanks in the United States.

Pilgrims and Native Americans give thanks for enough food.

Timeline

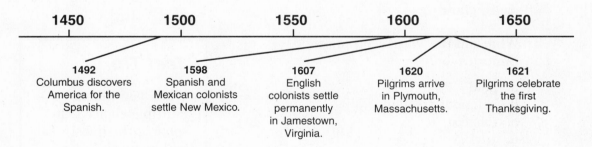

1450	1500	1550	1600	1650

1492
Columbus discovers America for the Spanish.

1598
Spanish and Mexican colonists settle New Mexico.

1607
English colonists settle permanently in Jamestown, Virginia.

1620
Pilgrims arrive in Plymouth, Massachusetts.

1621
Pilgrims celebrate the first Thanksgiving.

Getting Information from the Reading

A. Choose the best answer for each of these questions. Fill in the correct circle on the answer sheet to the right. The first one is done for you.

1. When did Christopher Columbus discover America?

   a. 1400
   b. 1492
   c. 1600
   d. 1692

2. Colonists from England first came to America in the

   a. 1400s.
   b. 1500s.
   c. 1600s.
   d. 1700s.

3. What was the first permanent English colony called?

   a. Plymouth
   b. Jamestown
   c. Native America
   d. England

4. What did the Pilgrims come to America for?

   a. gold
   b. religious freedom
   c. tobacco
   d. turkey

5. What was the first American holiday?

   a. Thanksgiving
   b. Independence Day
   c. Christmas
   d. Memorial Day

6. On what ship did the Pilgrims come to America?

   a. *Pinta*
   b. *Mayflower*
   c. *Virginia*
   d. *Plymouth*

Answer Sheet

1. (a) ● (c) (d)

2. (a) (b) (c) (d)

3. (a) (b) (c) (d)

4. (a) (b) (c) (d)

5. (a) (b) (c) (d)

6. (a) (b) (c) (d)

Test Tip

When you take a multiple-choice test, some of the questions will be hard. Put a small mark by the questions that you cannot answer the first time. Then, when you have answered most of the other questions, go back and look at those that you marked. If you are still not sure of the answer, GUESS.

B. Write the correct word or words in each blank to complete the sentences below. Use the words listed in the box on page 11. You may not use all of the words in the box. The first one is done for you.

1. ___Spices___ are used to season food.

2. Tobacco was one of the first _____ grown in the English colonies.

3. _____ is a very smooth fabric.

4. Columbus and a group of _____ crossed the Atlantic.

5. English _____ traded tobacco with England.

6. _____ means to find for the first time.

7. To _____ in a place means to move there and make it your permanent home.

8. When travelers _____ their destination, they have arrived at the place they set out for.

C. Discuss these questions with a partner or group.

1. Look at a map of the world. Which parts of the map show the New World?

2. Are there native people in your country? What were their lives like in the past? What are their lives like now?

3. Do you have Native American heritage? What do you know about it?

4. The first Europeans came to North America for work and for religious freedom. Do people still come to the United States for the same reasons? Who?

The N-400 Application: Part 4

Part 4. Information about your residences and employment.

A. List your addresses during the last five (5) years or since you became a permanent resident, whichever is less. Begin with your current address. If you need more space, continue on separate paper.

Street Number and Name, City, State, Country, and Zip Code	Dates (month/day/year)	
	From	To

B. List your employers during the last five (5) years. List your present or most recent employer first. If none, write "None". If you need more space, continue on separate paper.

Employer's Name	Employer's Address	Dates Employed (month/day/year)		Occupation/position
	Street Name and Number - City, State and ZIP Code	From	To	

THE INS INTERVIEW

A. Practice this dialogue with a partner.

INS: Please remain standing and raise your right hand. Do you promise to tell the truth and nothing but the truth, so help you God?
You: Yes, I do.
INS: Do you swear that all the information on your application, the documents you submitted, and the information you give today is the truth?

You: Yes, I do.
INS: You may sit down. Do you understand what an oath is?
You: Yes, it's like a promise to tell the truth.
INS: Right.

INS: You are here for your naturalization interview. Why do you want to be a U.S. citizen?
You: Because I want to bring my parents here, and I want to be able to vote.

INS: We're going to go over your application to see if there are any changes. Do you still live at the same address?
You: No, I've moved. My new address is 1234 Oak Street.
INS: When did you move to that address?
You: October 1st.

INS: Do you still work for the same employer?
You: Yes, I do.
INS: How long have you worked there?
You: For three years.
INS: Do you still have the same position?
You: I'm sorry. I don't understand.
INS: Do you still have the same job?
You: Oh, yes. I'm still a machine operator.

B. Now practice the dialogue using correct information about yourself.

C. If you take the history and government test at the INS interview, these are some of the questions you might be asked. Practicing the answers to these questions will help you remember the facts.

1. Why did the Pilgrims come to America?

2. Who helped the Pilgrims in America?

3. What is the name of the ship that brought the Pilgrims to America?

4. Which holiday was celebrated for the first time by the American colonists?

5. What is the most important right granted to U.S. citizens?

Christopher Columbus lands in North America in 1492.

GETTING TO KNOW ENGLISH

The Verb *Be*

The verb *be* is a very important verb in English. We use it in a lot of sentences. *Be* can also be a difficult verb. It is often irregular or different from other verbs.

Present Tense of the Verb *Be*

We use the present tense of *be* (*am*, *are*, or *is*) when we are talking about things that are always true. For example:

> She *is* smart.
> The world *is* round.
> I *am* a U.S. citizen.
> Many people *are* naturalized citizens.

I *am*	I *am* not
You *are*	You *are* not (aren't)
He *is*	He *is* not (isn't)
She *is*	She *is* not (isn't)
It *is*	It *is* not (isn't)
We *are*	We *are* not (aren't)
They *are*	They *are* not (aren't)

Past Tense of *Be*

We use the past tense of *be* (*was* or *were*) when we are talking about things that were always true in the past. For example:

> My mother *was* a Mexican citizen.
> Christopher Columbus *was* an explorer.
> The parents of many U.S. citizens *were* immigrants.

I *was*	I *was* not (wasn't)
You *were*	You *were* not (weren't)
He *was*	He *was* not (wasn't)
She *was*	She *was* not (wasn't)
It *was*	It *was* not (wasn't)
We *were*	We *were* not (weren't)
They *were*	They *were* not (weren't)

 A. Use the correct form of the present tense of the verb *be* in these sentences. The first one is done for you.

1. Jamestown _____*is*_____ in Virginia.

2. Spain and England _____ in Europe.

3. Thanksgiving _____ celebrated on the fourth Thursday in November.

4. The *Mayflower* _____ the ship that brought the Pilgrims to America.

5. Turkey, sweet potatoes, and corn _____ foods we eat on Thanksgiving.

B. Use the correct form of the past tense of the verb *be* in these sentences. The first one is done for you.

1. Some people thought that Christopher Columbus _____*was*_____ crazy.

2. The new land Columbus discovered _____ in the Caribbean Sea.

3. The Pilgrims _____ colonists who wanted religious freedom.

4. Jamestown, Virginia, _____ the first permanent English colony in North America.

5. The Pilgrims _____ thankful for the help of the Native Americans.

C. Present tense or past tense? Work with a partner to answer these questions. Make sure that you use the correct form of the verb *be*.

1. What is your name?

2. What is your current address?

3. What was your address before that?

4. When did you move from your last address?

5. Where were you born?

6. What was the date you became a permanent resident?

7. Who is your current employer?

8. Who was your employer before that?

9. What is your employer's address?

10. When did you work for your last employer?

11. What is your occupation?

12. What was your port of entry?

CHAPTER 3

A New Nation Is Born

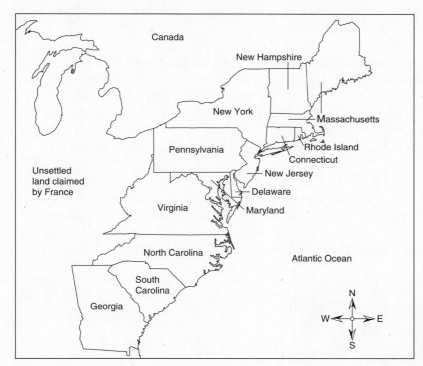

Thirteen colonies declared their independence from England in 1776.

Getting into the Reading

1. What is a colony?

2. Why do you think a colony might want independence?

3. Was your native country a colony? If so, which country ruled it?

4. Are you an independent person? Do you think that it is good or bad to be independent? Why?

Words to Know

battle	continental	pursuit
commander-in-chief	goods	representation
congress	obey	tax

Revolution and Independence

England had thirteen colonies along the Atlantic, or eastern seacoast of North America. They were New Hampshire, Massachusetts, Rhode Island, Connecticut, New York, New Jersey, Pennsylvania, Delaware, Maryland, Virginia, North Carolina, South Carolina, and Georgia. These colonies later became the first thirteen states.

The colonists had to obey the laws of the king of England. Because of these laws, the colonists could not trade with other countries. They had to send the goods they produced to England, and they could buy goods only from England. The colonists had to pay high taxes to England. They did not have any representation—anyone to act or speak for them—in England to control how much tax was charged or how the tax money was used. They had taxation without representation.

Many colonists did not like these laws. When the king put a high tax on tea, the colonists in Boston, Massachusetts, got angry. Some of them dressed like Native Americans to disguise themselves and threw the tea from a ship in Boston Harbor into the water. This event was called the Boston Tea Party.

Young lawyer Patrick Henry speaks out against laws of the King of England.

Thomas Jefferson was the main author of the Declaration of Independence.

People from the colonies got angry. Representatives from each colony met in Philadelphia, Pennsylvania, in 1774. This meeting was called the First Continental Congress. The representatives decided (1) to ask the king to change some of his laws, (2) to end all trade with England, and (3) to prepare for war. In March 1775, Patrick Henry said, "Give me liberty or give me death" at a meeting in Virginia.

In May 1775, the colonists had a Second Continental Congress at Independence Hall in Philadelphia, Pennsylvania. The representatives decided that they wanted to be independent from England. They asked Thomas Jefferson to write the Declaration of Independence.

On July 4, 1776, representatives of all thirteen colonies signed the Declaration of Independence. It says that "all men are created equal" and have rights that government cannot take away. These rights are "life, liberty, and the pursuit of happiness." People tell the government what to do, and the government must do what the people say. The Declaration of Independence says the colonists decided to be "free and independent states." The 4th of July is now called Independence Day, the birthday of the United States.

A picture of George Washington appears on every U.S. dollar bill.

The Revolutionary War, or the War of Independence, began in 1775 and ended in 1783. George Washington was the commander-in-chief of the colonial army and navy. He won many battles against the English. The colonists won the war, and the United States became an independent country.

In 1789, George Washington became the first president of the United States. When he died, he was known as "the father of his country."

Timeline

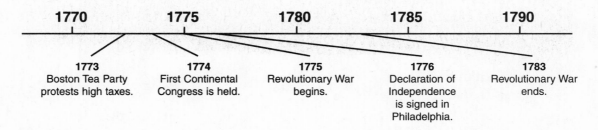

1770	1775	1780	1785	1790

1773	1774	1775	1776	1783
Boston Tea Party protests high taxes.	First Continental Congress is held.	Revolutionary War begins.	Declaration of Independence is signed in Philadelphia.	Revolutionary War ends.

The U.S. Flag

The U.S. flag has thirteen red and white stripes. They represent the first thirteen colonies. It has fifty white stars on a blue background. The stars represent the fifty states. Because of its design, the flag is often called the "Stars and Stripes."

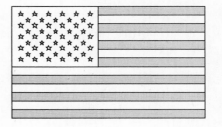

Getting Information from the Reading

A. Choose the best answer for each of these questions. Fill in the correct circle on the answer sheet below. The first one is done for you.

1. The thirteen colonies were located near the

    a. Pacific seacoast.
    b. Atlantic seacoast.
    c. Midwest.
    d. Southwest.

2. What was the Boston Tea Party a protest against?

    a. communism
    b. Native Americans
    c. religious freedom
    d. high taxes

3. Who was the main writer of the Declaration of Independence?

    a. Thomas Jefferson
    b. Patrick Henry
    c. George Washington
    d. Martin Luther King

4. In the Revolutionary War, the colonists fought against

    a. France.
    b. Germany.
    c. England.
    d. Russia.

5. During which war was George Washington the commander-in-chief?

    a. World War I
    b. World War II
    c. Revolutionary War
    d. Civil War

6. Who was the first president of the United States?

    a. Thomas Jefferson
    b. Patrick Henry
    c. George Washington
    d. Martin Luther King

7. How many stripes are on the American flag?

    a. 12
    b. 13
    c. 50
    d. 100

Answer Sheet

1. ⓐ ● ⓒ ⓓ

2. ⓐ ⓑ ⓒ ⓓ

3. ⓐ ⓑ ⓒ ⓓ

4. ⓐ ⓑ ⓒ ⓓ

5. ⓐ ⓑ ⓒ ⓓ

6. ⓐ ⓑ ⓒ ⓓ

7. ⓐ ⓑ ⓒ ⓓ

B. Write the correct word or words in each blank to complete the sentences below. Use the words listed in the box on page 21. You may not use all of the words in the box. The first one is done for you.

1. The thirteen original colonies had to _____*obey*_____ the laws of the king of England.

2. The colonists traded tobacco that they produced for tea and other _____ produced by England.

3. The president of the United States is also called the _____ _____ of the armed forces.

4. The colonists were angry because they had no _____ in England; that is, they had no one to help decide how to spend tax money.

5. Other colonists were angry because the _____ on the goods they produced was not fair.

6. People have the right to "life, liberty, and the _____ of happiness."

7. In the Revolutionary War, the Americans won many _____, but they also lost many others.

C. Discuss these questions with a partner or group.

1. England wanted the colonists to buy products from only that country. Why do you think the English wanted that? How would you feel if someone said you could buy things only at one store?

2. The colonists in North America were unhappy living in a colony. Do you think it is possible for people to live happily in any country that is a colony of a more powerful country? Why?

3. Why do we pay taxes when we buy things? How does the government use our tax money? What can we do if we think the taxes are unfair?

4. Does your native country celebrate an independence day? If so, how? How do you celebrate the 4th of July?

5. What does your native country's flag look like? What do the colors and symbols on it represent?

The N-400 Application: Part 5

Part 5. Information about your marital history.

A.   Total number of times you have been married _____ . If you are now married, complete the following regarding your husband or wife.

Family name	Given name	Middle initial

Address		

Date of birth (month/day/year)	Country of birth	Citizenship

Social Security#	A# (if applicable)	Immigration status (If not a U.S. citizen)

Naturalization (If applicable)
(month/day/year) _____   Place   (City, State) _____

If you have ever previously been married or if your current spouse has been previously married, please provide the following on separate paper: Name of prior spouse, date of marriage, date marriage ended, how marriage ended and immigration status of prior spouse.

THE INS INTERVIEW

A. Practice this dialogue with a partner.

INS: Now we're going to go over your application to see if there are any changes since you submitted it. Is your address still the same?
You: Yes, it is.
INS: You have been a permanent resident since 1985?
You: Yes, I have.
INS: Are you currently married?
You: No, I'm not. I am divorced.

INS: For how long were you married?
You: Six years.
INS: Did you live with each other from the time you were married until the time you were divorced?
You: I don't understand.
INS: You lived together the whole time?
You: Oh. Yes, we did.
INS: Why did you get divorced?
You: We had problems.

INS: You have been absent from the United States how many times since you got your permanent residence?
You: I went on vacation to Mexico two times.
INS: When?
You: Last year I was gone for three weeks.
INS: And before that?
You: I went the year before for three weeks, too.

B. Now practice the dialogue using correct information about yourself.

Dictation Tip

Sometimes when we speak, we do not say every word clearly. Listen carefully to this sentence. How many words did you hear? _____ Listen again. This time write the words you hear.

_____

Look carefully at what you wrote. Which words are missing? Listen carefully again. Did you hear more words? Write them.

_____

C. During the INS interview, the interviewer will read a sentence to you. You then must write the sentence correctly in English. Practice by listening carefully and writing the sentences that you hear. The first one is done for you.

1. _George Washington was the first president._____

2. _____

3. _____

4. _____

5. _____

"The Star-Spangled Banner"

"The Star-Spangled Banner" is our national anthem. The words are from a poem by Francis Scott Key. He wrote the song after watching an attack by the English on a U.S. fort during the War of 1812. The morning after the attack, he saw the American flag still flying. He knew the Americans had won.

Americans show love for their country in many ways. At special events and sports games, they raise the flag and sing the national anthem.

GETTING TO KNOW ENGLISH

Yes/No Questions and Short Answers

Yes/no questions are questions that can be answered *yes* or *no*. For example:

Are you married?
Yes, I am.   No, I am not. (No, I'm not.)

Some of the questions that you will be asked in the INS interview are yes/no questions. Many of the answers to these questions, like the one above, will use a form of the verb *be* (*am*, *are*, or *is*).

A. Answer these questions with a short answer using a form of the verb *be*. The first one is done for you.

1. Are you married? <u>Yes, I am.   No, I am not.</u>

2. Are you a permanent resident? _____

3. Is your wife a U.S. citizen? _____

4. Are you living in Houston now? _____

5. Were you born in Poland? _____

Other questions will use other verbs, such as *do* or *can*. If you listen carefully to the question, you will know which verb to use. For example:

Do you want to become a U.S. citizen?
Yes, I do.   No, I do not. (No, I don't.)

Can you read and write English?
Yes, I can.   No, I cannot. (No, I can't.)

B. Practice answering these questions with a short answer. Make sure that you use the correct verb in your answer. The first one is done for you.

1. Do you work for ABC Industries now? <u>Yes, I do.   No, I do not (don't).</u>

2. Can you read this paper? _____

3. Do you swear to tell the whole truth? _____

4. Did you live in Boston for two years? _____

5. Do your children live with you? _____

6. Do you have your social security card with you? _____

7. Did you return to the United States from Mexico by car? _____

C. Ask a partner the questions below. Then answer your partner's questions.

1. Is your family name Smith?

2. What is your middle initial?

3. What is your middle name?

4. You were born in 1962?

5. What is your date of birth?

6. Is Mexico your native country?

7. Do you live in Chicago?

8. What is your mailing address?

9. Are you a permanent resident?

10. Where did you enter the United States?

11. Can you speak, read, and write English?

12. You are married?

13. Do you want to change your name?

14. You are a citizen of which country?

15. Did you leave the United States since you became a permanent resident?

16. Tell me about the times you left the United States since you became a permanent resident.

17. Why did you leave the United States?

18. What is your current address?

19. Are you currently employed?

20. How long have you worked there?

21. When did you start work there?

22. Do you swear to tell the truth and nothing but the truth, so help you God?

CHAPTER 4

Civil War and Expansion

Without immigrants, there would be no United States of America.
Most immigrants were happy for new opportunities. Some,
like slaves, did not choose to come here.

Getting into the Reading

1. What are some reasons immigrants come to the
   United States today?

2. What were some reasons in the past?

3. What is a civil war?

4. Why are civil wars very difficult for a country?

5. The United States expanded in the 1800s. What does that mean?

Words to Know

agriculture	captured	federal	rapidly
assassinated	crowded	industry	separate
bloody	economy	plantation	slave
border	expanded	prohibit	treaty

Abraham Lincoln and the Civil War

Africans came to the United States during the same period of time as the first colonists did. The colonists came as free people. Africans came as slaves. They were captured from their homes in Africa and were brought in crowded ships. Hundreds of thousands of Africans died before they reached America.

Slaves had to work long hours with no hope of freedom or of going home. They were the property of their owners. Many slaves worked on plantations to produce cotton and tobacco. In 1860, there were four million slaves—one out of every seven Americans.

Southern states allowed slavery; Northern states did not. The Southern states wanted to continue slavery, but many people in the North wanted to end it. Some people in the South also disliked slavery. The Southern states thought the state governments should be allowed to decide whether or not to allow slavery.

Also, the economy of the South was based largely on agriculture, and the North on industry. The South thought the federal government made policies that helped the Northern economy but hurt the Southern economy. The Southern states decided to separate from the United States. The Northern states did not want them to separate.

The Civil War was fought between the Northern states and the Southern states from 1861 to 1865. The Northern states were called the Union, and the Southern states were called the Confederacy.

President Abraham Lincoln was the commander-in-chief of the army that saved the Union. Lincoln was against slavery. After he became president in 1861, eleven states left the Union and formed the Confederacy. In 1863, Lincoln signed a document called the Emancipation Proclamation. It freed most of the slaves. African Americans were allowed to join the Union Army. Lincoln was assassinated soon after the Civil War ended.

The North won the war in 1865, and the North and the South became one country again. The Civil War was very bloody; more than half a million Americans died. After the Civil War, the 13th amendment was added to the Constitution to prohibit slavery.

Timeline

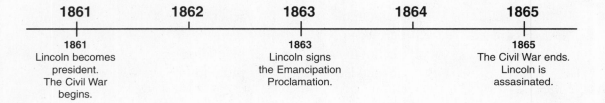

1861	1862	1863	1864	1865
1861 Lincoln becomes president. The Civil War begins.		1863 Lincoln signs the Emancipation Proclamation.		1865 The Civil War ends. Lincoln is assasinated.

Moving West

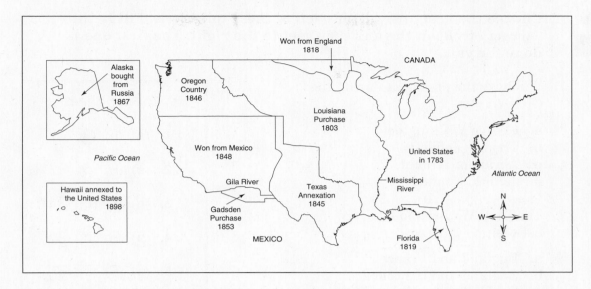

When George Washington became the first president, the United States was much smaller than it is today. The western border of the United States was the Mississippi River.

In the 1800s, the United States expanded to the Pacific Ocean. The government bought the Louisiana Territory from France and got Florida from Spain. After war with Mexico, the Southwest (including California) became part of the United States. So did Texas. The United States signed a treaty with England for the Oregon Country in the Northwest. The United States bought Alaska from Russia and took control of Hawaii. Alaska and Hawaii were the last states to join the union.

The population of the United States grew rapidly as it expanded to the West. Immigrants made up a large part of the people needed to help the United States grow. From the 1800s to the 1960s, most immigrants came from Europe. Today's immigrants come largely from Latin America and Asia.

Timeline

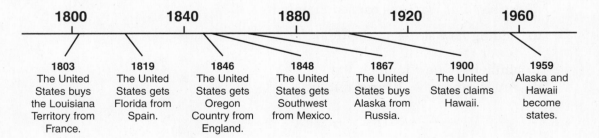

Getting Information from the Reading

A. Choose the best answer for each of these questions. Fill in the correct circle on the answer sheet to the right. The first one is done for you.

1. Who was the president during the Civil War?

   a. George Washington
   b. Thomas Jefferson
   c. Abraham Lincoln
   d. John F. Kennedy

2. The Civil War was fought between

   a. England and France.
   b. England and the colonies.
   c. the Union and the Confederacy.
   d. Japan and Germany.

3. Which side won the Civil War?

   a. the North
   b. the South
   c. the Colonists
   d. the English

4. Which were the last two states to join the Union?

   a. Virginia and Massachusetts
   b. Alaska and Hawaii
   c. California and Texas
   d. Washington and Oregon

5. The rapid increase in the U.S. population after the Civil War was caused mainly by

   a. adding new states to the union.
   b. fewer men lost in battle.
   c. millions of new immigrants.
   d. Americans having large families.

Answer Sheet

1. ⓐ ⓑ ● ⓓ

2. ⓐ ⓑ ⓒ ⓓ

3. ⓐ ⓑ ⓒ ⓓ

4. ⓐ ⓑ ⓒ ⓓ

5. ⓐ ⓑ ⓒ ⓓ

B. Match each word on the left with a word on the right that means the OPPOSITE by drawing a line between them. The first one is done for you.

1. a slave
2. a plantation
3. to prohibit
4. to expand
5. to capture
6. to be assassinated
7. agriculture
8. federal
9. to separate

a. to be born
b. industry
c. a free person
d. state
e. to unite
g. to allow
h. to shrink
i. to free
j. a factory

 C. Answer these questions orally.

1. What were some of the reasons for the Civil War?

2. Was there slavery in your country? If so, what do you know about it? How did it end?

3. Was there a civil war in your country? If so, who fought?

4. Was your country always the same size? If not, how did it grow or get smaller?

5. What did you learn about how the Southwest became part of the United States? How do you feel about that?

6. Where did most immigrants come from in the past? Why?

7. Where do most immigrants come from today? Why?

The N-400 Application: Part 6

Part 6. Information about your children.

B. Total Number of Children _____ Complete the following information for each of your children. If the child lives with you, state "with me" in the address column; otherwise give city/state/country of child's current residence. If deceased, write "deceased" in the address column. If you need more space, continue on separate paper.

Full name of child	Date of birth	Country of birth	Citizenship	A - Number	Address

THE INS INTERVIEW

A. Practice this dialogue with a partner.

INS: Are you currently married?
You: Yes, I am.
INS: For how long have you been married?
You: Six years.

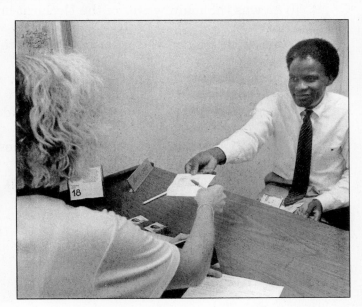

INS: Before that?
You: I was married before.
INS: What happened?
You: We got a divorce. Here is the divorce paper, the decree.
INS: Was your first wife a U.S. citizen?
You: Yes, she was.
INS: Did you marry her to get your green card?
You: No. I married her because I loved her.

INS: On your application for permanent residence, you said you had three children. Now you have four children listed. Why?
You: My second wife and I had a child together. I had three children with my first wife.
INS: Do they all live with you?
You: The three children from my first marriage live with my first wife. Our child lives with us.
INS: Do you have evidence of child support?
You: Yes. Here are copies of my money orders.

B. Now practice the dialogue using correct information about yourself.

C. If you take the U.S. history and government test at the INS interview, you will be asked some of these questions from the INS List of 100 Questions.

1. Who said "Give me liberty or give me death"?

2. Which country did we fight during the Revolutionary War?

3. Who was the main writer of the Declaration of Independence?

4. When was the Declaration of Independence adopted?

5. What is the basic belief of the Declaration of Independence?

6. What is the date of Independence Day? Independence from whom?

7. Can you name the thirteen original colonies?

8. Which president is called "the father of our country"?

9. What is the national anthem of the United States?

10. Who wrote "The Star-Spangled Banner"?

11. Who was president during the Civil War?

12. What did the Emancipation Proclamation do?

13. Which president freed the slaves?

14. What are the colors of our flag?

15. How many stripes are there on the flag?

16. What do the stripes on the flag mean?

17. How many stars are there on our flag?

18. What do the stars on the flag mean?

19. What is the 49th state added to our Union?

20. What is the 50th state added to our Union?

21. Who was the first president of the United States?

22. How many states are there in the Union?

23. What were the original thirteen states of the United States called?

GETTING TO KNOW ENGLISH

Past Tense

When we talk about something that we do every day, or something that is always true, we use the <u>present</u> tense. For example:

 You *work* very hard.   Immigrants *arrive* every day.

When we talk about something that happened in the past we use the <u>past</u> tense. For example:

 Slaves *worked* very hard.   You *arrived* three years ago.

Past Tense of Regular Verbs

The past tense of regular verbs is formed by adding *ed* or *d* to a verb.

A. Write the past tense of the verb in parentheses. The first one is done for you.

 1. Many slaves died before they (reach) _____*reached*_____ America.

 2. The Southern states (call) _____ themselves the Confederacy.

 3. The Southern states (want) _____ to continue slavery.

 4. The Civil War (end) _____ slavery in the United States.

Spelling of Past Tense Verbs

Sometimes the spelling of a verb is different when you add *ed* for the past tense. There are three rules to remember:

 a. If a word ends in an *e*, just add *d*.
   arrive + *d* = arrived
 b. If a word ends in *y*, change the *y* to *i* and add *ed*.
   study + *ed* > studied
 c. If a verb has one syllable and ends in a vowel (*a, e, i, o, u*) and one consonant, double the consonant and add *ed*.
   stop + *p* + *ed* = stopped

B. Practice forming the past tense of these verbs. Be careful of your spelling. The first one is done for you.

 1. Lincoln (stop) _____*stopped*_____ slavery in the United States.

 2. Lincoln (save) _____ the Union.

 3. The 13th Amendment (end) _____ slavery.

 4. The borders of the United States (expand) _____ in the 1800s.

5. The North (worry) _____ that slavery was not right.

6. Lincoln (sign) _____ the Emancipation Proclamation.

7. African Americans (join) _____ the Union Army.

8. Many slaves (work) _____ in the production of cotton.

Past Tense of Irregular Verbs

There are many irregular verbs in the past tense. You cannot just add *ed* to the ends of these verbs to form the past tense. There is no easy way to remember these verbs, so you will need to study them carefully.

C. **Practice forming the past tenses of regular and irregular verbs. The first one is done for you.**

1. Slave ships (bring) _____*brought*_____ many slaves here.

2. The North (fight) _____ the South during the Civil War.

3. Many people in the South (think) _____ slavery was OK.

4. The policies of the federal government (hurt) _____ the South.

5. The South (decide) _____ to separate from the Union.

6. The United States (buy) _____ the Louisiana Territory from France.

7. Hawaii and Alaska (become) _____ states in 1959.

8. The Civil War (be) _____ very bloody.

9. Eleven states (leave) _____ the Union.

D. **Ask a partner the questions below. Then answer your partner's questions. Make sure you use the past tense correctly.**

1. When did you come to the United States?

2. Why did you come to the United States?

3. Where did you work last year?

4. When did you last leave the United States?

5. Where did you go when you left?

6. When did you return?

CHAPTER 5

The World Goes to War

Soldiers leaving for war say goodbye to their friends and families.

Getting into the Reading

1. How do you think the soldiers in the pictures above feel?
2. What is a world war?
3. How many world wars have there been? Why did people fight these wars?
4. What happened in your native country during the world wars?
5. What do you know about the Vietnam War? the Korean War? the Cold War?
6. Have you ever been a soldier? Did you fight in a war? If so, what was it like?

Words to Know

atomic bombs	democratic	resolve	troops
combat	Great Depression	stock market	warships
communist	international	submarine	weapons
defeated	public service	tank	

World War I and the Great Depression

World War I began in 1914 and ended in 1918. Thirty countries fought in World War I. It was the first war that used such modern weapons as airplanes, tanks, and submarines.

The United States entered World War I after German warships attacked American ships in 1917. The United States helped England, France, Russia, and other countries win the war. They defeated a group of nations led by Germany and Austria-Hungary. When the war ended, the United States had become a world power.

After World War I, the U.S. economy did well until the Great Depression from 1929 to 1939. The Depression was a very difficult time. Many people lost their jobs or had their salaries cut. Business after business closed, and people lost their homes and farms. Many people lost money in the stock market.

Franklin Roosevelt was president during much of the Depression. He helped make public service jobs for the unemployed with a program called the New Deal. People built roads, parks, bridges, and buildings for the government. President Roosevelt gave the people new hope.

Timeline

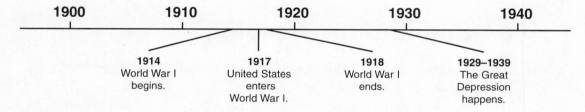

| 1900 | 1910 | 1920 | 1930 | 1940 |

1914
World War I
begins.

1917
United States
enters
World War I.

1918
World War I
ends.

1929–1939
The Great
Depression
happens.

Tanks, first used in World War I, roll off to battle.

World War II

World War II began in 1939 when Germany invaded Poland. Germany was led by Adolf Hitler. Japan and Italy joined to fight on the side of Germany. The group was called the Axis countries.

The United States entered the war after Japanese planes bombed Pearl Harbor in Hawaii in 1941. More than 2,000 Americans died there. The United States joined the Allied countries, which included the United Kingdom, France, Canada, Australia, New Zealand, Russia, and China.

The Allies defeated Germany following the famous D-Day invasion in Normandy, France, in 1944. Japan surrendered after the United States dropped two atomic bombs on Hiroshima and Nagasaki in 1945. The United States and the Soviet Union became the two major world powers after World War II.

World War II was a terrible experience. More than 22 million people died. Many countries came together after the war to form a new international organization called the United Nations (UN). The UN helps countries to discuss and resolve, or find an answer to, world problems and occasionally to take action. It also gives many countries economic help.

American soldiers land in Normandy, France, during the D-Day invasion in June 1944.

The Cold War

A new kind of war, the Cold War, began after World War II. Countries with different political and economic systems are not often friendly toward each other. The Cold War was between the United States and the Soviet Union and other communist countries. They had very different political and economic systems.

The United States and Western Europe were democratic, and the Soviet Union and much of Eastern Europe were communist. A democracy permits private ownership of property; a communist government does not. Also in a democracy, all people are part of the government. In a communist state, only a few people run the government.

The communist and democratic countries competed with each other for political support and economic markets. There was no combat, but the countries were cold toward each other. By the late 1980s, the Soviet Union and other communist countries were moving toward democracy. The Cold War ended in 1991 when these countries voted to give up communism.

Timeline

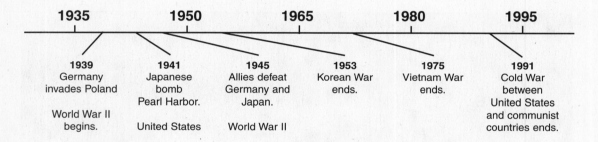

| 1935 | 1950 | 1965 | 1980 | 1995 |

1939
Germany invades Poland

World War II begins.

1941
Japanese bomb Pearl Harbor.

United States

1945
Allies defeat Germany and Japan.

World War II

1953
Korean War ends.

1975
Vietnam War ends.

1991
Cold War between United States and communist countries ends.

Wars in Asia

From 1950 to 1953, the United States fought to protect non-communist South Korea from communist North Korea in the Korean War. At the end of the war, Korea remained divided.

The United States tried to defeat communism in Vietnam, too. From 1964 to 1973, U.S. troops supported South Vietnam against North Vietnam in the Vietnam War. North Vietnam won the war and united the country under its leadership.

Timeline

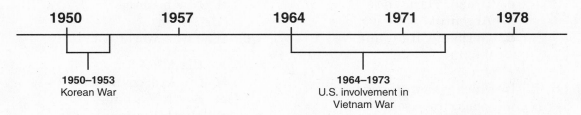

| 1950 | 1957 | 1964 | 1971 | 1978 |

1950–1953
Korean War

1964–1973
U.S. involvement in
Vietnam War

U.S. troops fight a losing battle in Vietnam.

Getting Information from the Reading

 A. Choose the best answer for each of these questions. Fill in the correct circle on the answer sheet below. The first one is done for you.

1. Which were the Axis countries during World War II?

   a. Vietnam, Laos, and Cambodia
   b. United States, England, and the Soviet Union
   c. Brazil, Peru, and Argentina
   d. Germany, Italy, and Japan

2. In which war were modern weapons first used?

   a. World War I
   b. World War II
   c. Korean War
   d. Vietnam War

3. The Great Depression occurred between

   a. the Civil War and World War I.
   b. World War I and World War II.
   c. World War II and the Korean War.
   d. the Korean War and the Vietnam War.

4. The United Nations (UN) was founded to

   a. help countries discuss and resolve world problems.
   b. provide education and economic aid.
   c. occasionally take action.
   d. all of the above

5. Which country did the United States support in the Vietnam War?

   a. South Vietnam
   b. South Korea
   c. North Vietnam
   d. North Korea

6. Who won World War II?

   a. the Allies
   b. the Axis countries
   c. South Vietnam
   d. North Vietnam

Answer Sheet

1. ⓐ ⓑ ⓒ ●
2. ⓐ ⓑ ⓒ ⓓ
3. ⓐ ⓑ ⓒ ⓓ
4. ⓐ ⓑ ⓒ ⓓ
5. ⓐ ⓑ ⓒ ⓓ
6. ⓐ ⓑ ⓒ ⓓ

B. Write the correct word or words in each blank to complete the sentences below. Use the words listed in the box on page 41. You may not use all of the words in the box. The first one is done for you.

1. _____*Troops*_____ is another name for soldiers.

2. Examples of modern weapons include _____

    _____ , _____, and

    _____.

3. People can own property and be part of a _____
   form of government.

4. A _____ government, run by only a few people,
   does not permit private ownership of property.

5. The United Nations helps to _____ world problems and also
   provides economic help.

6. _____ means many countries working together.

C. Answer these questions orally. Use short answers.

1. After World War I ended, the United States was a world power. What
   does that mean? Why was the United States considered a world power?
   How did that change after World War II?

2. In your country, what did you learn about the Cold War between the
   United States and the Soviet Union?

3. Many people in the United States protested the war in Vietnam. Why
   did they protest? Do you think they were right or wrong?

Mississippi protesters against the Vietnam war march in the 1960s.

Review:

U.S. Department of Justice
Immigration and Naturalization Service

START HERE - Please Type or Print

Part 1. Information about you.

Family Name	Given Name	Middle Initial

U.S. Mailing Address - Care of

Street Number and Name		Apt. #
City	County	
State	ZIP Code	

Date of Birth (month/day/year)	Country of Birth
Social Security #	A #

Part 2. Basis for Eligibility *(check one).*

a. ☐ I have been a permanent resident for at least five (5) years .

b. ☐ I have been a permanent resident for at least three (3) years and have been married to a United States Citizen for those three years.

c. ☐ I am a permanent resident child of United States citizen parent(s) .

d. ☐ I am applying on the basis of qualifying military service in the Armed Forces of the U.S. and have attached completed Forms N-426 and G-325B

e. ☐ Other. (Please specify section of law) _____ .

Part 3. Additional information about you.

Date you became a permanent resident (month/day/year)	Port admitted with an immmigrant visa or INS Office where granted adjustment of status.
Citizenship	

Name on alien registration card (if different than in Part 1)

Other names used since you became a permanent resident (including maiden name)

Sex ☐ Male ☐ Female	Height	Marital Status: ☐ Single ☐ Married	☐ Divorced ☐ Widowed

Can you speak, read and write English ? ☐No ☐Yes.

Absences from the U.S.:

Have you been absent from the U.S. since becoming a permanent resident? ☐ No ☐Yes.

If you answered **"Yes"** , complete the following, Begin with your most recent absence. If you need more room to explain the reason for an absence or to list more trips, continue on separate paper.

Date left U.S.	Date returned	Did absence last 6 months or more?	Destination	Reason for trip
		☐ Yes ☐ No		
		☐ Yes ☐ No		
		☐ Yes ☐ No		
		☐ Yes ☐ No		
		☐ Yes ☐ No		
		☐ Yes ☐ No		

Form N-400 (Rev. 07/17/91)N *Continued on back.*

THE INS INTERVIEW

A. Practice this dialogue with a partner.

INS: Is your name Martínez Peter?
You: Yes.
INS: Are you sure?
You: Well, no. It's Peter Martínez.
INS: Do you want to change your name legally when you become a citizen?
You: No.

INS: When did you get your permanent residency?
You: In 1989.
INS: But you say you have two children born in Mexico, one in 1990 and one in 1994. Why is that?
You: My wife stays in Mexico sometimes.
INS: Did you leave the United States in 1990 and 1994 to visit your wife?
You: Yes, I did.
INS: Did you stay for more than six months?
You: No. Well, in 1994, I stayed seven months.
INS: Did you get permission to return from the INS?
You: Yes, I did.
INS: Did you return as a permanent resident and enter with your permanent resident card?
You: Yes, I did.

INS: Did you originally enter the United States through New York City?
You: No, I didn't. I entered through Chicago.
INS: When was that?
You: In 1989.

B. Now practice the dialogue using correct information about yourself.

Dictation Tip

When we speak English, we do not always speak clearly. Sometimes we combine two words so that they sound like one word. Listen carefully to this sentence. How many words did you hear? _____

Listen again and write down the words you hear.

_____

Look carefully at what you wrote. Think about the beginnings and endings of the words. Is the end of one word combined with the beginning of the next word so that it sounds like one word, or like a different word? Listen carefully again. Write down the words you hear.

_____

C. During the INS interview, the interviewer will read a sentence to you. You then must write the sentence correctly in English. Practice by listening carefully and writing the sentences that you hear. The first one is done for you.

1. *The United States is made up of fifty states.*

2. _____

3. _____

4. _____

5. _____

D. If you take the U.S. history and government test at the INS interview, you will be asked some of these questions from the INS List of 100 Questions.

1. Name one purpose of the United Nations.

2. Which countries were our allies during World War II?

GETTING TO KNOW ENGLISH

Past Tense Questions and Short Answers

We often answer questions with short answers. The verbs in the answers are usually the same as those in the questions. For example:

> Is he Mexican? Yes, he is.
> Was she born in 1956? No, she wasn't.
> Do you speak English? Yes, I do.

In the past tense, questions are often made with the past tense of *do*, which is *did*. When we answer these questions, we also use the word *did*. For example:

> Did you study history? Yes, I did.
> Did your children come with you to the United States? Yes, they did.

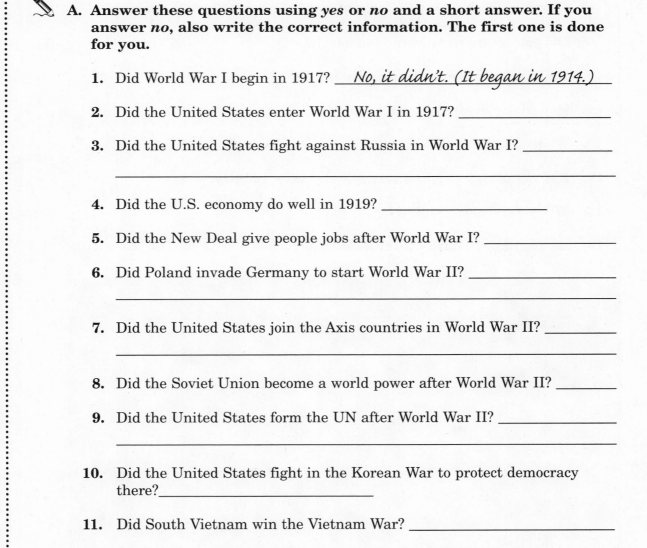

A. Answer these questions using *yes* or *no* and a short answer. If you answer *no*, also write the correct information. The first one is done for you.

1. Did World War I begin in 1917? *No, it didn't. (It began in 1914.)*

2. Did the United States enter World War I in 1917? _____

3. Did the United States fight against Russia in World War I? _____

_____

4. Did the U.S. economy do well in 1919? _____

5. Did the New Deal give people jobs after World War I? _____

6. Did Poland invade Germany to start World War II? _____

_____

7. Did the United States join the Axis countries in World War II? _____

_____

8. Did the Soviet Union become a world power after World War II? _____

9. Did the United States form the UN after World War II? _____

_____

10. Did the United States fight in the Korean War to protect democracy there?_____

11. Did South Vietnam win the Vietnam War? _____

12. Did your native country fight in World War I or II? _____

13. Did the Cold War end in 1981? _____

B. In your INS interview, many of the questions will begin with the word *did*. Other questions will be information questions in the present or past tense. Practice answering these questions with a partner.

1. Did you become a permanent resident five years ago?

2. Did you leave the United States last year?

3. Did you return by car?

4. Did your absence last for six months or more?

5. Have you lived at your current address for the last five years?

6. Have you worked for your current employer for the last five years?

7. Did you get married more than once?

8. Did your spouse ever get married before?

9. How many children do you have?

10. Where do your children live?

11. Did any of your children stay in your native country?

12. When were your children born?

13. Do any of them have U.S. citizenship?

CHAPTER 6

The Constitution:
Supreme Law of the Land

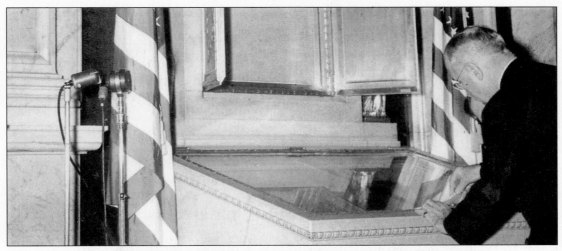

President Harry S. Truman views the U.S. Constitution at the National Archives in Washington, D.C.

Getting into the Reading

1. What is a law? Can you give some examples of laws in the United States?

2. What is a constitution? Does your native country have a constitution?

3. What do you know about the U.S. Constitution?

4. The U.S. Constitution says that people have certain rights. What is a right? Can you give some examples of rights that people have in the United States?

Words to Know

amendment	discrimination	power
branch	introduction	ratified
checks and balances	philosophy	supreme

The U.S. Constitution

The Constitution is the highest law of the United States. All people and all laws must follow the Constitution. It is the supreme law of the land.

In 1787, the Constitution was written at a meeting in Independence Hall in Philadelphia, Pennsylvania. Two years later, in 1789, the Constitution was approved, or ratified. Although the United States has changed a lot since then, the Constitution is still the foundation for our government.

The first part of the Constitution is called the Preamble. The Preamble is the introduction to the Constitution. It sets forth the purpose and basic beliefs, or philosophy, of our government—a government by the people.

The second part of the Constitution, the seven articles, includes a description of the three branches of our government. These separate areas of power are the executive branch, the legislative branch, and the judicial* branch. The executive branch includes the president, vice president, and cabinet. The legislative branch includes the U.S. Congress. The judicial branch includes the Supreme Court and lower federal courts.

Each branch of government has different powers so that no one person, group, or branch of government has too much power. This is called a system of checks and balances. For example, the Supreme Court (judicial) can overturn, or "check," the power of Congress (legislative); Congress can overturn, or "check," the power of the president (executive), and so on, to keep a balance of power among all three branches.

The last part of the Constitution is the amendments. Amendments are the changes made since the Constitution was written. To change the Constitution, the government must vote to add an amendment. The first ten amendments are called the Bill of Rights. There is a total of 27 amendments. The newest amendment was added in 1992.

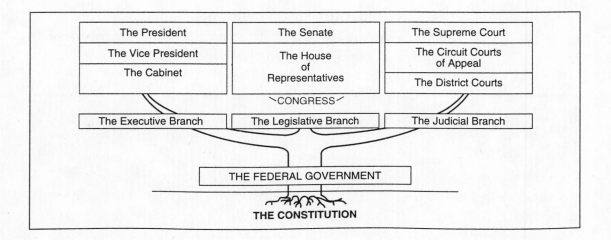

Getting Information from the Reading

 A. Write the correct word or words in each blank to complete the sentences below. Use the words listed in the box on page 53. You may not use all of the words in the box. The first one is done for you.

1. The courts are part of the judicial _____*branch*_____ of government.

2. The Preamble to the Constitution introduces the _____ of the U.S. government.

3. In the United States, the Constitution is the _____ law of the land.

4. The Constitution was _____ in 1789.

5. The system of _____ guarantees that no branch of government has more power than any other branch.

 B. Answer these questions orally. Use short answers.

1. Why is the Constitution called the "supreme law of the land"?

2. Why are there three branches in the U.S. government? Which countries have governments with only one or two branches?

Martin Luther King, Jr.

Martin Luther King, Jr., was an African American minister who worked to end discrimination against minorities in the 1960s.

Because of his work, laws were passed that helped protect the rights of all people. For example, the Twenty-fourth Amendment to the Constitution says that no one has to pay tax in order to vote. All citizens, rich or poor, can vote.

In 1964, King won the Nobel Peace Prize. He was assassinated in Memphis, Tennessee, in 1968.

The Bill of Rights

The Bill of Rights was added to the Constitution in 1791. These rights and freedoms are guaranteed to all people in the United States.

Amendment 1: <u>Freedom of Speech:</u> People can say what they want.
<u>Freedom of Press:</u> People can print or broadcast what they want.
<u>Freedom of Religion:</u> People can practice any religion they want.
<u>Freedom of Peaceable Assembly:</u> People can gather together peacefully to request changes in the government.

Amendment 2: People can own guns, with some limits as to use.

Amendment 3: The government cannot force people to keep soldiers in their homes when there is no war.

Amendment 4: The government cannot search or take a person's property without a warrant, or order, from a court.

Amendment 5: A person cannot be tried for the same crime twice. A person cannot be forced to testify against her- or himself. People accused of crimes have the right to fair legal treatment.

Amendment 6: A person charged with a crime has the right to a trial by jury and to have a lawyer.

Amendment 7: People in civil lawsuits have the right to a fair trial by a jury in most cases.

Amendment 8: People cannot be charged very high fines (bonds) or be given cruel punishment by the government.

Amendment 9: People have other rights in addition to those in the Constitution.

Amendment 10: Any power that does not belong to the federal government belongs to the states or to the people.

Getting Information from the Reading

A. Write the correct word or words in each blank to complete the sentences below. Use the words listed in the box on page 56. You may not use all of the words in the box. The first one is done for you.

1. A person convicted of a _____*crime*_____ is called a criminal.

2. The police need a _____ to go to a person's house to search for stolen things.

3. The newspapers _____ stories, and television stations _____ news about crimes in the area.

4. People charged with a crime are _____ in a court of law.

5. Usually, there are twelve people in a court who make up the _____.

6. During a _____, people _____ and tell what they know about the crime.

7. Lawyers can ask a person to testify about what happened, but they cannot _____ a person to testify against him- or herself.

8. People who disobey the law sometimes have to pay a _____, and sometimes the _____ is to be sent to jail.

9. Everyone has rights that are _____ under the Constitution.

B. Answer these questions orally. Use short answers.

1. Which rights guaranteed by the Bill of Rights are most important to you? What rights do you have in your native country?

2. What rights that are not part of the Bill of Rights do you think should be included?

3. Here are some other important amendments to the Constitution and the years they were added. What other amendments do you think should be made to the Constitution?

   Amendment 13: Ended slavery in the United States (1865).
   Amendment 14: Guaranteed citizenship to all people born or naturalized in the United States (1868).
   Amendment 15: Gave people of all races the right to vote (1870).
   Amendment 19: Gave women the right to vote (1920).
   Amendment 26: Gave eighteen-year-olds the right to vote (1971).

C. Choose the best answer for each of these questions. Fill in the correct circle on the answer sheet below. The first one is done for you.

1. What are the first ten amendments to the Constitution called?

    a. Bill of Rights
    b. Preamble
    c. amendments
    d. executive branch

2. The Constitution is called the

    a. judicial branch.
    b. executive branch.
    c. supreme law of the land.
    d. Supreme Court.

3. The Nineteenth amendment, which gave women the right to vote, was added in

    a. 1776.
    b. 1853.
    c. 1920.
    d. 1976.

4. Which of the following is NOT in the Bill of Rights?

    a. Freedom of speech
    b. Freedom of religion
    c. Right to trial by jury
    d. Right to free medical care

5. What is a change to the Constitution called?

    a. the Preamble
    b. an amendment
    c. the Bill of Rights
    d. an article

6. How many branches are there of the federal government?

    a. 1
    b. 2
    c. 3
    d. 4

7. Martin Luther King was a famous

    a. president.
    b. baseball player.
    c. civil rights leader.
    d. general in the army.

Answer Sheet

1. ● ⓑ ⓒ ⓓ

2. ⓐ ⓑ ⓒ ⓓ

3. ⓐ ⓑ ⓒ ⓓ

4. ⓐ ⓑ ⓒ ⓓ

5. ⓐ ⓑ ⓒ ⓓ

6. ⓐ ⓑ ⓒ ⓓ

7. ⓐ ⓑ ⓒ ⓓ

The N-400 Application: Part 7 (Questions 1–3)

Some of these questions are difficult to understand. Below are the questions and some simple explanations that might help. If you are not sure about your answer, use a dictionary to help you understand more of the words.

It is important that you answer these questions honestly. The INS can check your information to see if you are being honest. If you answer "yes" to any of these questions, you should get legal advice.

> 1. Are you now, or have you ever been a member of, or in any way connected or associated with the Communist Party, or ever knowingly aided or supported the Communist Party directly, or indirectly through another organization, group or person, or ever advocated, taught, believed in, or knowingly supported or furthered the interests of communism?   ☐ Yes ☐ No

Explanation: Have you ever been a member of the Communist Party or helped the Communist Party in any way?

> 2. During the period March 23, 1933 to May 8, 1945, did you serve in, or were you in any way affiliated with, either directly or indirectly, any military unit, paramilitary unit, police unit, self-defense unit, vigilante unit, citizen unit of the Nazi party or SS, government agency or office, extermination camp, concentration camp, prisoner of war camp, prison, labor camp, detention camp or transit camp, under the control or affiliated with:
>   a. The Nazi Government of Germany?   ☐ Yes ☐ No
>   b. Any government in any area occupied by, allied with, or established with the assistance or cooperation of, the Nazi Government of Germany?   ☐ Yes ☐ No

Explanation: Were you a member of the Nazi Party between 1933 and 1945, or did you help the Nazi government in any way?

> 3. Have you at any time, anywhere, ever ordered, incited, assisted, or otherwise participated in the persecution of any person because of race, religion, national origin, or political opinion?   ☐ Yes ☐ No

Explanation: Did you ever punish or hurt a person because of his or her race, religion, national origin, or political opinion?

> ### Good Moral Character
>
> The INS wants to be sure that people applying for U.S. citizenship are of good moral character. You do <u>not</u> have good moral character if you:
> - lied to the INS when you got your permanent residence.
> - did not file federal tax returns every year as a permanent resident.
> - have committed certain crimes.
> - have been involved in illegal activity.
> - were a member of the Communist or Nazi Party.
> - got married just to get your permanent residence.
> - did not register with the Selective Service (men born after 1960 who lived in the United States between the ages of 18 and 25).
>   See the appendix for more information.

THE INS INTERVIEW

A. You may not understand every question the INS interviewer asks you. Here are some things you might want to say if you don't understand.

I'm sorry. Could you repeat that?
I didn't understand what you said. Could you say it again?
Excuse me? I'm not sure what you mean.
I'm sorry. Could you say that more slowly?
I'm sorry. Do you mean _____ or _____ ?

B. Practice this dialogue with a partner.

INS: You were a member of the Communist Party, weren't you?
You: Yes. In Poland. I had to join the party to go to the university.
INS: You didn't believe in communism but you had to join the party?
You: I didn't understand what you said. Could you say it again?
INS: Sure. Do you believe in communism now?
You: No, I don't.

C. Now practice the dialogue with correct information about yourself. Tell the interviewer in different ways that you do not understand the question.

D. If you take the U.S. history and government test at the INS interview, you will be asked some of these questions from the INS List of 100 Questions.

1. What is the supreme law of the United States?

2. What is the introduction to the Constitution called?

3. In what year was the Constitution written?

4. How many branches are there in our government? What are the branches of our government called?

5. Can the Constitution be changed? What do we call a change to the Constitution?

6. How many changes or amendments are there to the Constitution?

7. What are the first ten amendments to the Constitution called?

8. Whose rights are guaranteed by the Constitution and Bill of Rights?

9. Name one right guaranteed by the first amendment.

10. Who was Martin Luther King, Jr.?

GETTING TO KNOW ENGLISH

Tag Questions

Sometimes, when we think we know the answer but are not sure, we ask a question with a tag on the end. These kinds of questions seem more polite or less embarrassing than more direct information questions. When the INS interviewer asks you questions about your application, he or she might use some of these tag questions. The information is on the application, but the interviewer wants to make sure the information is true. For example:

You are a Mexican citizen, *aren't you*?
You have six children living with you, *don't you*?

The first part and the last part of tag questions do not seem to agree. One part is positive (+), and the other part is negative (-). For example:

You've been married twice, haven't you?
    (+)   (-)
You didn't leave the country for more than six months, did you?
    (-)   (+)

When you answer a tag question, listen to the first part of the question. That is what the person thinks is true. Your answer will tell the person if that part is true or not. If the information in the first part of the question is not correct, you should give the correct information. For example:

You've been married two times, haven't you?
    Yes, I have. / No, I haven't. I've been married once.
You aren't married, are you?
    Yes, I am. I got married last month. / No, I'm not.

 A. Practice answering these questions. The first one is done for you.

1. You're applying to be a naturalized citizen, aren't you?

   Yes, I am. / No, I'm not.

2. Your port of entry was New York, wasn't it?

   _____

3. You've filed a tax return every year, haven't you?

   _____

4. You haven't been arrested, have you?

   _____

B. Now answer these questions about the Bill of Rights and other amendments. Write the number of the amendment that gives us this right. The first one is done for you.

1. People in the United States can own guns, can't they?

   _Yes, they can._____ Amendment: ___2___

2. Poor people can't have a lawyer if they don't have any money, can they?

   _____ Amendment: _____

3. The police can come into your home any time, can't they?

   _____ Amendment: _____

4. The government can try you twice for the same crime, can't they?

   _____ Amendment: _____

5. Any kind of punishment is OK for criminals, isn't it?

   _____ Amendment: _____

6. I can practice any religion I want, can't I?

   _____ Amendment: _____

7. Newspapers are allowed to print anything they want, aren't they?

   _____ Amendment: _____

8. The police can make you testify against yourself, can't they?

   _____ Amendment: _____

9. People in the United States can have slaves, can't they?

   _____ Amendment: _____

10. You have to be twenty-one years old to vote, don't you?

    _____ Amendment: _____

CHAPTER 7

The Executive Branch of Government

Each of these men was president of the United States.

Getting into the Reading

1. How many of the men in the pictures above do you recognize? What are their names?

2. Who are the current president and vice president of the United States?

3. Who is the leader of your native country? Is the leader called a president or something else?

4. How is the leader of your native country chosen?

5. What do you think are qualities of a good leader?

Words to Know

advise	campaign	enforce	requirement
appointed	candidate	inaugurated	responsibilities
bill	Democratic	nominate	term of office
cabinet	elects	Republican	veto

The Executive Branch

The executive branch of the federal government includes the president, the vice president, the cabinet, and the departments led by cabinet members. The executive branch enforces, or makes people obey, laws and puts new laws into effect.

The president is the leader of the executive branch. Sometimes called the chief executive officer of the United States, the president enforces the law. The president signs bills, or ideas for new laws, and makes them laws. The president can veto, or turn down, a bill if he or she does not agree with it. The president is also the commander-in-chief of the United States Army and Navy (armed forces).

The White House is the president's official home. It is located at 1600 Pennsylvania Avenue, N.W., in Washington, D.C.

According to the Constitution, a person must meet certain requirements, or necessary things, to become president. The person must be at least 35 years old, be born a U.S. citizen (not a naturalized citizen), and must have lived in the United States for at least 14 years.

Every four years, the United States elects a president for a four-year term of office. He or she can serve no more than two full terms (eight years).

The president is elected on the first Tuesday in November and is inaugurated, or put into office, in January. The people do not elect the president; they elect the electoral college representatives for each candidate. The candidate, or person who wants to be elected, with the most votes in a state gets all of the electoral votes for that state. Then, the electoral college elects the president.

The vice president has special responsibilities, or duties, which are listed in the Constitution. He or she becomes president if the president dies or quits. The vice president must meet the same requirements for office as the president.

The cabinet is appointed by the president. The executive branch of government has 14 departments. The leaders of these departments are appointed by the president and form the president's cabinet. The 14 cabinet members meet with and advise the president, helping him or her run these important areas of government. Most cabinet members are called secretaries. For example, there is a Secretary of Defense, a Secretary of Health and Human Services, and others.

Presidents' Day

George Washington was born on February 22. Abraham Lincoln was born on February 12. Today we honor them both by celebrating Presidents' Day on the third Monday in February.

Political Parties

People who agree on how the government should be run form groups called political parties. In the United States, the two main political parties are the Democratic Party and the Republican Party. These two parties have different ideas about government and how it should work.

Before a presidential election, both of these parties have their own national convention. Party members make a list, called a platform, of the political ideas they think are important for the next four years. They decide who, from the leaders in their party, they want to be president. Then the parties choose, or nominate, one Democratic and one Republican candidate for president. Both candidates campaign in every state. They try to convince people to vote for them, and they make promises about what they will do as president.

In the election, there are always at least two candidates for president. Usually, candidates from smaller political parties also run for president.

Democrats

Many Democrats believe that the government has a responsibility to help people. They want to do this through such social and economic programs as unemployment insurance, national health care, literacy programs, and programs to protect the rights of women and minorities.

Recent Democratic presidents:

William Clinton
Jimmy Carter
Lyndon Johnson
John Kennedy

Republicans

Many Republicans believe that people should help themselves. They think the government should do only the things that individuals cannot do for themselves, such as have military forces to protect the United States. Republicans also believe in less government interference in business and state activities.

Recent Republican presidents:

George Bush
Ronald Reagan
Richard Nixon
Dwight Eisenhower

Where to Write to the President

President _____ , The White House, 1600 Pennsylvania Avenue, N.W., Washington, D.C. 20500.

Getting Information from the Reading

A. Choose the best answer for each of these questions. Fill in the correct circle on the answer sheet below. The first one is done for you.

1. How many terms can a president serve?

   a. one
   b. two
   c. three
   d. for life

2. Which of these is NOT a requirement to be president?

   a. 35 years old
   b. U.S.-born citizen
   c. male
   d. U.S. resident for at least 14 years

3. Who elects the president?

   a. the people
   b. the executive branch
   c. the Supreme Court
   d. the electoral college

4. Who makes up the executive branch of government?

   a. president, vice president, cabinet, and the departments under the cabinet members
   b. president and first lady
   c. Senate and House of Representatives
   d. Democrats and Republicans

5. The cabinet

   a. is appointed by the president.
   b. advises the president.
   c. includes the Secretary of Defense and the Secretary of Health and Human Services.
   d. all of the above

6. What is the president's official home called?

   a. Green House
   b. White House
   c. Capitol
   d. State House

7. Which national holiday celebrates the birthdays of Washington and Lincoln?

   a. Thanksgiving
   b. Independence Day
   c. Memorial Day
   d. Presidents' Day

Answer Sheet

1. (a) ● (c) (d)
2. (a) (b) (c) (d)
3. (a) (b) (c) (d)
4. (a) (b) (c) (d)
5. (a) (b) (c) (d)
6. (a) (b) (c) (d)
7. (a) (b) (c) (d)

B. Write the correct word or words in each blank to complete the sentences below. Use the words listed in the box on page 63. You may not use all of the words in the box. The first one is done for you.

1. The United States _____*elects*_____ a president every four years, in November.

2. Before a person can become president, a political party must _____ him or her as a candidate.

3. The president can sign a bill into law and _____ it or _____ a bill he or she does not agree with.

4. The cabinet members _____ the president about his or her _____ to the country.

5. In a U.S. presidential election, there is always one _____ candidate and one _____ candidate.

6. Being a U.S.-born citizen is one _____ for a person who wants to become president.

7. A president may quit before his or her _____ is finished.

C. Answer these questions orally. Use short answers.

1. Which of these qualities do you think is important for the president of the United States?
   Should be friendly.
   Should be trustworthy.
   Has to put good leaders in the cabinet.
   Must have good ideas and fight to put them in place.
   Should be able to listen to a lot of different opinions and then make a decision that includes many of the ideas.
   Should be a strong leader in world politics.
   Should be a strong leader in his or her political party.
   Has to be a good friend to people like you.
   Should agree with you on important things.

2. What do you like about the current president of the United States? What do you dislike about the current president?

3. Are the things that people in your native country expect from their leaders different from what people expect in the United States? If so, what are they?

✎ The N-400 Application: Part 7 (Questions 4–9)

Some of these questions are difficult to understand. Below are the questions and some simple explanations that might help. If you are not sure about your answer, use a dictionary to help you understand more of the words.

It is important for you to answer these questions honestly. The INS can check your information to see if you are being honest. If you answer "yes" to any of these questions, you should get legal advice.

4. Have you ever left the United States to avoid being drafted into the U.S. Armed Forces?	☐ Yes ☐ No

Explanation: Did you ever leave the United States so that you wouldn't have to be in the United States military (for men only)?

5. Have you ever failed to comply with Selective Service laws? If you have registered under the Selective Service laws, complete the following information: Selective Service Number:_____ Date Registered:_____ If you registered before 1978, also provide the following: Local Board Number:_____ Classification:_____	☐ Yes ☐ No

Explanation: Certain men have to register for the U.S. military. See the appendix for more information about who must register. If you were supposed to register, did you disregard that law?

6. Did you ever apply for exemption from military service because of alienage, conscientious objections or other reasons?	☐ Yes ☐ No

Explanation: Did you ever ask to stay out of the U.S. military because of your religious beliefs or for other reasons (for men only)?

7. Have you ever deserted from the military, air or naval forces of the United States?	☐ Yes ☐ No

Explanation: Did you ever leave the U.S. military when you were not supposed to?

8. Since becoming a permanent resident , have you ever failed to file a federal income tax return ?	☐ Yes ☐ No

Explanation: Since becoming a permanent resident, did you ever NOT file federal income tax returns?

9. Since becoming a permanent resident , have you filed a federal income tax return as a nonresident or failed to file a federal return because you considered yourself to be a nonresident?	☐ Yes ☐ No

Explanation: Since becoming a permanent resident, did you ever say that you were a nonresident on your income tax form?

THE INS INTERVIEW

A. Practice this dialogue with a partner.

INS: Did you register for the Selective Service?
You: I don't know. I think so.
INS: Do you know your selective service number?
You: No.
INS: Here's a telephone number. You'll have to call this number to get your selective service number.
You: Now?
INS: Yes, and then we can continue.

INS: Did you get the information?
You: Yes. My number is 71-13000815-4. I registered on May 30, 1992.
INS: Okay.

INS: Do you file your tax returns every year?
You: Yes, I do.

B. Now practice the dialogue with correct information about yourself.

C. During the INS interview, the interviewer will read a sentence to you. You then must write the sentence correctly in English. Practice by listening carefully and writing the sentences that you hear. The first one is done for you.

1. _The vice president works in Washington, D.C._

2. _____

3. _____

4. _____

5. _____

6. _____

7. _____

8. _____

President Clinton signs a bill into law.

D. Sometimes in the interview you might need more time to think of the answer to a question. Other times you might not know the complete answer. Here are some things you might want to say.

Hmmm . . .
Let me see . . .
Can I think about that for a minute? I think I know the answer.
I don't remember that answer. Can you ask me another question?
I don't know the answer, but I do know . . .
I studied everything, but I forgot that answer.

E. If you take the U.S. history and government test at the INS interview, you will be asked some of these questions from the INS List of 100 Questions. If you need to have the question repeated, need more time, or know only part of the answer, be sure to say that.

1. What is the executive branch of our government?

2. Who is the president of the United States today?

3. Who is the vice president of the United States today?

4. What is the name of the president's official home?

5. Where is the White House?

6. Who elects the president of the United States?

7. For how long does the United States elect its president?

8. How many full terms can a president serve?

9. In which month do U.S. citizens vote for the president?

10. In which month is the president inaugurated?

11. According to the U.S. Constitution, a person must meet certain requirements in order to be eligible to become president. Name one of these requirements.

12. Who becomes president of the United States if the president should die?

13. Who signs bills into law?

14. What special group advises the president?

15. Who is the commander-in-chief of the United States Army and Navy?
    Who was the first commander-in-chief of the United States armed forces?

GETTING TO KNOW ENGLISH

Can, Should, Had Better, Must, and Have To

Sometimes we use "helping verbs" to express our ideas. *Can*, *should*, *had better*, *must*, and *have to* are some of these helping verbs. For example:

> The president can sign laws into effect.

Can means he or she has the ability to do this: he or she is able to do this.

> The president should be a good citizen.
> The president had better make good decisions.

Should and *had better* mean that this is good advice. If the president is smart, he or she will do these things.

> The president must be at least 35 years old.
> The president has to be a U.S.-born citizen.

Must and *have to* mean that this is necessary; it is required.

When we use these helping verbs in sentences, they are followed by the simple form of a verb. For example:

> We should *vote* in every election.
> We must *file* an income tax return every year.
> We have to *pay* a fee with our N-400.

 A. Fill in the blanks with *can*, *should*, *had better*, *must*, or *have/has to*. The first one is done for you.

1. People in the United States _____*can*_____ say what they want.

2. Citizens _____ be eighteen years old to vote.

3. A person who wants to become president _____ be a good leader.

4. Citizens _____ vote for the best candidate for president.

5. A candidate for president _____ be a U.S.-born citizen.

6. The president _____ serve only two terms.

B. Work with a partner to answer these questions. Use complete sentences, and be sure that you use the correct form of the verb.

1. Name one thing you should be honest about on your N-400.
2. Name one thing you can do in the United States because of the Bill of Rights.
3. Name one thing you must not do if you want to become a naturalized citizen of the United States.

CHAPTER 8

The Legislative Branch of Government

José López Portillo, former President of Mexico, addresses the U.S. Congress.

Getting into the Reading

1. What does the legislative branch of government do?

2. What are members of Congress called?

3. What is the building in which they work called?

4. What are the names of your senators and representatives in Congress?

5. Who is the current Speaker of the House of Representatives?

Words to Know

amend	defeated	majority	two-thirds majority
committee	district	pass	veto
debate	legislation		

The Legislative Branch

The legislative branch of the U.S. government spends most of its time passing legislation, or making laws. It also has the power to declare war.

The legislative branch of the federal government is the Congress of the United States. Congress has two parts, or houses. One house is called the House of Representatives, and the other is called the Senate. Both houses meet in the Capitol Building in Washington, D.C.

There are 100 members of the Senate. Each of the 50 states has two representatives called senators, so each state has equal power in the Senate. Senators serve a six-year term and represent their whole state. There is no limit to the number of times a senator can be reelected. The vice president is the leader of the Senate.

There are 435 members of the House of Representatives. The population of a state determines the number of representatives for that state. Every state has at least one representative; some states have more than 25. Each representative, elected by a district (an area) of his or her state, represents the people of that district. Representatives serve a two-year term. There is no limit to the number of times a representative can be reelected.

The leader of the House of Representatives is called the Speaker of the House. The Speaker, who is elected by the House members, becomes the president of the United States if both the president and the vice president die or leave office.

Senators and representatives serve the people they represent. They listen to the people they represent and make decisions on how to vote on bills. They also decide which bills they might want to put forth, or introduce. People can give their thoughts and ideas by calling or writing their senators and representatives.

Your senators and representatives have offices in your state and in Washington, D.C. Staff members in these offices can help you with federal law issues, such as immigration, social security, income tax, and public housing.

Where to Write to a Member of Congress

Senator _____
U.S. Senate
Washington, D.C. 20510

Representative _____
U.S. House of Representatives
Washington, D.C. 20515

How a Bill Becomes a Law

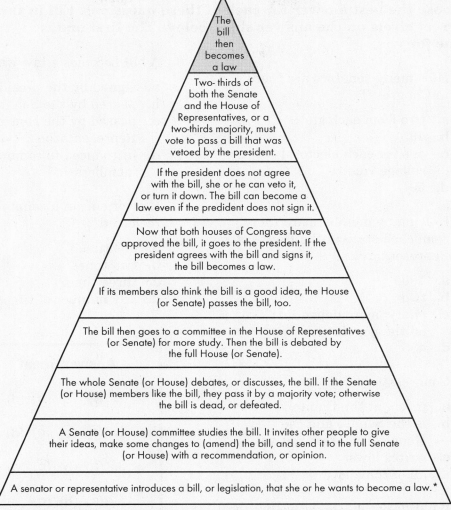

The bill then becomes a law

Two-thirds of both the Senate and the House of Representatives, or a two-thirds majority, must vote to pass a bill that was vetoed by the president.

If the president does not agree with the bill, she or he can veto it, or turn it down. The bill can become a law even if the predident does not sign it.

Now that both houses of Congress have approved the bill, it goes to the president. If the president agrees with the bill and signs it, the bill becomes a law.

If its members also think the bill is a good idea, the House (or Senate) passes the bill, too.

The bill then goes to a committee in the House of Representatives (or Senate) for more study. Then the bill is debated by the full House (or Senate).

The whole Senate (or House) debates, or discusses, the bill. If the Senate (or House) members like the bill, they pass it by a majority vote; otherwise the bill is dead, or defeated.

A Senate (or House) committee studies the bill. It invites other people to give their ideas, make some changes to (amend) the bill, and send it to the full Senate (or House) with a recommendation, or opinion.

A senator or representative introduces a bill, or legislation, that she or he wants to become a law.*

Viewed from bottom to top, this diagram shows how a bill becomes a law.

IRCA: A Federal Law

In 1986, a law that affected many immigrants was passed by Congress and signed by the president. It is the Immigration Reform and Control Act of 1986 (IRCA), often called amnesty or legalization. IRCA gave legal status to many immigrants who did not have papers.

IRCA also requires employers to check that the people they hire are allowed to work in the United States legally. Employers can be fined for hiring people who do not have legal status.

* A bill can be introduced in either the Senate or the House of Representatives.

Getting Information from the Reading

 A. Choose the best answer for each of these questions. Fill in the correct circle on the answer sheet below. The first one is done for you.

1. How many senators are there in Congress?

    a. two from each state
    b. 435
    c. one for each electoral college vote
    d. 50

2. How many members are there from each state in the House of Representatives?

    a. 100
    b. two
    c. one or more depending on the population
    d. 435

3. Congress

    a. meets at the Capitol.
    b. is the Senate and the House of Representatives.
    c. writes laws.
    d. all of the above

4. What does the legislative branch of government do?

    a. makes laws
    b. interprets laws
    c. enforces laws
    d. violates laws

5. How long is a senator's term?

    a. two years
    b. four years
    c. six years
    d. eight years

6. A bill becomes a law when it is

    a. signed by the president.
    b. passed by the Senate.
    c. passed by the House of Representatives.
    d. introduced to committee members.

7. How often can a senator be reelected?

    a. one time
    b. two times
    c. three times
    d. any number of times

Answer Sheet

1. ● ⓑ ⓒ ⓓ

2. ⓐ ⓑ ⓒ ⓓ

3. ⓐ ⓑ ⓒ ⓓ

4. ⓐ ⓑ ⓒ ⓓ

5. ⓐ ⓑ ⓒ ⓓ

6. ⓐ ⓑ ⓒ ⓓ

7. ⓐ ⓑ ⓒ ⓓ

B. Write the correct word or words in each blank to complete the sentences below. Use the words listed in the box on page 73. You may not use all of the words in the box. The first one is done for you.

You are a congressional representative. In your _____*district*_____, there are many immigrants who want to become citizens. They want the INS to hire more naturalization officers so that people can become citizens faster. You decide to introduce _____ in the House of Representatives.

You give a great speech explaining your ideas to the House, and the bill goes to a _____ for study. They amend your bill and make a recommendation that the House pass the bill.

In the House, there is a long _____ about your bill. Some people really like it, but others do not. The House also amends your bill a little, but it finally passes by a _____ when the members vote. Your bill goes to the Senate.

After a Senate committee studies your bill, the committee members take it to the whole Senate. The Senate decides to _____ the bill and send it to the president.

The president knows that many of the people who voted for him like this bill. So he does not want to _____ it. He signs the bill into law.

C. Answer these questions orally. Use short answers.

1. How many representatives does your state have in the House of Representatives? What is the name of your representative? What party does he or she belong to?

2. What are your senators' names? What political party or parties do your senators belong to?

3. What do your congressional representatives think about these issues?
   a. gun control
   b. health care
   c. government benefits for poor people
   d. immigration

✎ The N-400 Application: Part 7 (Questions 10–15)

Some of these questions are difficult to understand. Below are the questions and some simple explanations that might help. If you are not sure about your answer, use a dictionary to help you understand more of the words.

It is important for you to answer these questions honestly. The INS can check your information to see if you are being honest. If you answer "yes" to any of these questions, you should get legal advice.

10	Are deportation proceedings pending against you, or have you ever been deported, or ordered deported, or have you ever applied for suspension of deportation?	☐ Yes ☐ No

Explanation: Have you ever been deported or ordered deported? Is the INS trying to deport you now?

11.	Have you ever claimed in writing, or in any way, to be a United States citizen?	☐ Yes ☐ No

Explanation: Did you ever say you were a U.S. citizen even though you were not?

12. Have you ever:		
a.	been a habitual drunkard?	☐ Yes ☐ No
b.	advocated or practiced polygamy?	☐ Yes ☐ No
c.	been a prostitute or procured anyone for prostitution?	☐ Yes ☐ No
d.	knowingly and for gain helped any alien to enter the U.S. illegally?	☐ Yes ☐ No
e.	been an illicit trafficker in narcotic drugs or marijuana?	☐ Yes ☐ No
f.	received income from illegal gambling?	☐ Yes ☐ No
g.	given false testimony for the purpose of obtaining any immigration benefit?	☐ Yes ☐ No

Explanation:
  a. Were you ever drunk every day?
  b. Were you ever married to more than one person at a time?
  c. Did you ever engage in sex for pay?
  d. Did you ever help someone enter the United States illegally?
  e. Did you ever sell narcotic drugs or marijuana?
  f. Did you ever get money illegally from gambling?
  g. Did you ever, under oath, lie at an INS interview or on an INS application?

13. Have you ever been declared legally incompetent or have you ever been confined as a patient in a mental institution? ☐ Yes ☐ No

Explanation: Were you ever in a mental hospital, or did a judge or court ever say you were legally incompetent?

14. Were you born with, or have you acquired in same way, any title or order of nobility in any foreign State? ☐ Yes ☐ No

Explanation: Are you a noble (king, queen, duke, earl, or other)?

15. Have you ever:
  a. knowingly committed any crime for which you have not been arrested? ☐ Yes ☐ No
  b. been arrested, cited, charged, indicted, convicted, fined or imprisoned for breaking or violating any law or ordinance excluding traffic regulations? ☐ Yes ☐ No

Explanation:
  a. Did you ever commit a crime for which you were not arrested?
  b. Have you ever been arrested for committing a crime, or for any reason?

THE INS INTERVIEW

A. Practice this dialogue with a partner.

INS: Why are you applying for naturalization?
You: Well, my parents are still in Mexico, and I want to bring them here. They are getting old, and I miss them.

INS: Have you ever been deported by immigration?
You: Yes, a long time ago.
INS: When?
You: Hmmmm . . . around 1979.
INS: Were you deported, or did you return to Mexico voluntarily?
You: I don't understand. Could you repeat that question?
INS: Did you have to go to court in front of a judge?
You: No. I was arrested at the border in California and returned to Mexico.
INS: Then it was a voluntary return. That's not a problem.

INS: Have you ever been arrested?
You: The police came to my house once because my husband and I were fighting. No charges were filed, so I didn't think it was important.
INS: Okay. You will have to go to the police station to get a letter saying you are in good moral standing.

INS: Any other arrests? The FBI will use your fingerprint chart to check for arrests, so you need to be sure.
You: I was arrested once for disorderly conduct.
INS: When was that?
You: A couple of years ago.
INS: We can't go on until I get a disposition from the court and a letter about your other arrest from the police station. We will send you a date for another interview.
You: I'm sorry. I didn't understand all of that. Could you say it again, more slowly?
INS: Sure. I need a record of your arrest from the court. I also need a letter from the police that says you are in good moral standing. You will need to come for another interview. We will send you another date. You must have all the information by then.
You: Could you write down what I need? Then I will have it all for sure.

B. Now practice the dialogue with correct information about yourself.

C. During the INS interview, the interviewer will read a sentence to you. You then must write the sentence correctly in English. Practice by listening carefully and writing the sentences you hear. The first one is done for you.

1. *Congress has two houses.*

2. _____

3. _____

4. _____

5. _____

D. If you take the U.S. history and government test at the INS interview, you will be asked some of these questions from the INS List of 100 Questions. If you need to have the question repeated, need more time, or know only part of the answer, be sure to say that.

1. What is the legislative branch of our government?

2. What is Congress?

3. What is the U.S. Capitol?

4. What is the duty of Congress?

5. Who has the power to declare war?

6. Who elects Congress?

7. Why are there 100 senators in the United States Senate?

8. For how long does each senator serve?

9. How many times may a senator be reelected?

10. Can you name the two senators from our state?

11. How many voting members are there in the House of Representatives?

12. For how long does each representative serve? How many times may a representative be reelected?

13. Who becomes president of the United States if the president and the vice president should die?

14. What are the two major political parties in the United States today?

GETTING TO KNOW ENGLISH

Articles

Articles are small English words, such as *a*, *an*, and *the*. When we speak, we do not always say them clearly. This sometimes makes listening (and dictations) difficult.

Here are some general rules for article use:

A and *an* are used only before singular nouns and only when talking about something in <u>general</u>. Use *a* before words beginning wth a consonant sound. For example:

A president should be smart.

Use *an* before words beginning with a vowel sound. For example:

An amendment is a change in the Constitution.

The is used when talking about a <u>specific</u> thing. Examples:

The president of the United States must be at least 35 years old.
The Thirteenth Amendment ended slavery in the United States.

Sometimes no article is used. That happens when we talk about something (a noun) that cannot be counted or the plural of something in general. Examples:

Presidents should be smart.
People can write to their senators and representatives.

 A. Practice using articles. Put *a*, *an*, *the*, or nothing in these blanks. The first one is done for you.

1. The president lives in ___*the*___ White House.

2. The president is _____ elected official.

3. _____ representatives can be reelected many times.

4. _____ responsibilities of a president are many.

5. The vice president serves _____ four-year term of office.

6. All people living in _____ America are protected by _____ Bill of Rights.

7. Washington, D.C., is _____ capital of _____ country.

8. Being a U.S.-born citizen is _____ requirement for the U.S. presidency.

CHAPTER 9

The Judicial Branch of Government

The U.S. Supreme Court is made up of nine judges, or justices.

Getting into the Reading

1. What is a judge? What does a judge do?

2. What are important qualities of a good judge?

3. Have you ever been to court in the United States? If so, what was it like?

4. What do you know about the Supreme Court?

5. What Supreme Court cases have you heard of?

Words to Know

appeal	hear	rights
case	interpreted	ruled
guilty	punishable by	system

The Judicial Branch

The judicial branch of government is a system of courts that hears cases and interprets, or explains, the laws. There are courts at the local, state, and federal levels. Each level is responsible for a different kind of case. For example, federal courts hear cases involving federal laws. State courts hear all other cases.

The highest court in the land is the U.S. Supreme Court. The Supreme Court decides if the Constitution permits certain laws. All other courts must follow the decisions of the U.S. Supreme Court. If a person loses a case in a lower federal court, he or she can appeal to, or ask, a higher-level federal court to hear the case. In the end, a case may go to the Supreme Court for a final decision.

There are nine justices on the Supreme Court. They are nominated by the president and must be approved by the Senate. Supreme Court justices are appointed to their jobs for life, or until they die. In 1981, Sandra Day O'Connor became the first female Supreme Court Justice. The leader of the Supreme Court is called the chief justice of the United States.

Visitors gather outside the Supreme Court building in Washington, D.C.

Gideon v. *Wainwright*

***Gideon* v. *Wainwright* was an important Supreme Court case.** Clarence Gideon was arrested for breaking into a building. He was poor, so he could not afford a lawyer. He wanted the court to give him one for free, but the judge said he had to pay because the crime was not punishable by death. Gideon had to be his own lawyer, but he did not do very well at the trial. The jury found him guilty.

Gideon believed that anyone who could be sentenced to at least one year in jail should have a lawyer, even if he or she could not afford to pay for one. While he was in jail, Gideon asked the Supreme Court to hear his case. In 1963, the Supreme Court agreed with Gideon. It said the Constitution guaranteed poor people the right to have a free lawyer in criminal cases.

Miranda v. *Arizona*

Another very important Supreme Court case was *Miranda* v. *Arizona*. Ernesto Miranda was arrested in Arizona for the rape of an 18-year-old girl. Police officers asked Miranda many questions, and he answered them without his lawyer there to help him. He then signed a paper that said he was guilty. At the trial, the jury decided he should be in prison for 20 to 30 years.

Miranda appealed his case to the Supreme Court. He believed the Constitution guaranteed him the right to be told he could have a lawyer present before the police asked him questions. The police officers had not told him that. In 1963, the Supreme Court ruled in favor of Miranda.

Now, because of these two cases, police officers must read people their rights when they are arrested for a criminal act. Below are the "Miranda Rights."

1) You have the right to be silent.
2) Anything you say can and will be used against you in court.
3) You have the right to talk to a lawyer before you answer questions.
4) You have the right to have a lawyer with you while you answer questions.
5) If you cannot afford a lawyer, you can have one free.

Getting Information from the Reading

A. Choose the best answer for each of these questions. Fill in the correct circle on the answer sheet below. The first one is done for you.

1. The judicial branch of the government is the
   a. Supreme Court and other courts.
   b. president, vice president, and the cabinet.
   c. Senate and House of Representatives.
   d. Democrats and Republicans.

2. The Supreme Court
   a. ignores the law.
   b. interprets the law.
   c. signs bills that become the law.
   d. makes laws.

3. How many members make up the Supreme Court?
   a. three
   b. six
   c. nine
   d. twelve

4. For how long do Supreme Court justices serve?
   a. two years
   b. four years
   c. six years
   d. for life

5. What is the leader of the U.S. Supreme Court called?
   a. president
   b. vice president
   c. chief justice
   d. speaker

Answer Sheet

1. ● ⓑ ⓒ ⓓ

2. ⓐ ⓑ ⓒ ⓓ

3. ⓐ ⓑ ⓒ ⓓ

4. ⓐ ⓑ ⓒ ⓓ

5. ⓐ ⓑ ⓒ ⓓ

Test Tip

On the standardized citizenship tests, you should always guess if you are not sure of an answer. There is no punishment for guessing wrong—and you might get the answer right.

B. Write the correct word or words in each blank to complete the sentences below. Use the words listed in the box on page 83. You may not use all of the words in the box. The first one is done for you.

In 1982, the Supreme Court heard *Pyler* v. *Doe*. This _____*case*_____ was about a law passed in the state of Texas. The law said that children of illegal aliens, or the undocumented, could not go to public school. The Supreme Court _____ the Constitution as saying that states <u>cannot</u> make laws to stop undocumented children from going to public schools. The court _____ that the Texas law was not constitutional.

In November 1994, people in California voted for Proposition 187. One part of this new law says that children who are undocumented cannot go to public schools in California. The courts have stopped the state of California from putting this part of Proposition 187 into effect because the case of *Pyler* v. *Doe* says this is not constitutional.

The state of California may want to take their case through the court _____ and _____ it to the Supreme Court, which may agree to _____ this case again. New justices have been appointed since 1982, and times have changed. The Supreme Court may change its ruling and say that states <u>can</u> stop undocumented children from going to school.

C. Work with a partner to answer these questions.

1. What are the names of the current Supreme Court justices? What is the name of the current chief justice?

2. The Miranda Rights are based on the Bill of Rights. Which amendments of the Bill of Rights are part of the Miranda Rights?

3. The Miranda Rights apply only to criminal law. What are some examples of criminal laws? Which kinds of arrests are not criminal?

The N-400 Application: Part 8

Simple Interpretation

I promise that:

    I do not have any loyalty to any other country;

    I believe in the Constitution and will defend it;

    I will be loyal to the United States;

    I will fight in the U.S. military in a national emergency when the law
        says I must;

    I will do non-fighting work (be a secretary, work in food service, etc.) for the
        U.S. military when the law says I must;

    I will do other work important for the country when the law says I must;
        and that

    I agree to this freely and without any doubts.

The Oath of Allegiance

I hereby declare, on oath, that I absolutely and entirely renounce and abjure all allegiance and fidelity to any foreign prince, potentate, state or sovereignty, of whom or which I have heretofore been a subject or citizen; that I will support and defend the Constitution and laws of the United States of America against all enemies, foreign and domestic; that I will bear true faith and allegiance to the same; that I will bear arms on behalf of the United States when required by the law; that I will perform noncombatant service in the armed forces of the United States when required by the law; that I will perform work of national importance under civilian direction when required by the law; and that I take this obligation freely without any mental reservation or purpose of evasion; so help me God.

THE INS INTERVIEW

 A. Practice this dialogue with a partner.

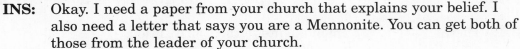

> **INS:** Do you know what the U.S. Constitution is?
> **You:** Yes. It is the basis for the government of the United States.
> **INS:** Do you believe in the Constitution and our form of government?
> **You:** Yes, I do.
>
> **INS:** If the government asked, would you bear arms or serve in the United States armed forces in another capacity?
> **You:** No. That is against my religion.
> **INS:** What is your religion?
> **You:** I am a Mennonite.
> **INS:** Okay. I need a paper from your church that explains your belief. I also need a letter that says you are a Mennonite. You can get both of those from the leader of your church.

B. Now practice the dialogue with correct information about yourself.

 C. During the INS interview, the interviewer will read a sentence to you. You then must write the sentence correctly in English. Practice by listening carefully and writing the sentences you hear.

1. _____

2. _____

3. _____

D. If you take the U.S. history and government test at the INS interview, you will be asked some of these questions from the INS List of 100 Questions. If you need to have the question repeated or need more time, say that.

1. What is the judicial branch of our government?

2. What are the duties of the Supreme Court?

3. How many Supreme Court justices are there?

4. Who nominates the Supreme Court justices?

5. Who is the chief justice of the Supreme Court?

GETTING TO KNOW ENGLISH

There Is/There Are

Often, when we want to describe something, we use the words *there is* or *there are*. For example:

There are thirteen stripes on the American flag.
There is one star on the flag for every state.

You have to decide whether to use *is* or *are*. Sometimes this is confusing in sentences with many extra words. These extra words are not important, but you have to know if the subject of the sentence is singular (one) or plural (more than one). For example:

(singular) There is <u>one</u> young, liberal, female senator who agrees.
(plural)   There are <u>50</u> little white stars on the flag.

 A. Write *is* or *are* in each of these sentences. Look carefully to decide if the word should be singular or plural. The first one is done for you.

1. There ____*are*____ 27 amendments to the Constitution.

2. There _____ ten amendments in the Bill of Rights.

3. There _____ three branches of the U.S. government.

4. There _____ one chief justice.

5. There _____ 435 members of the House of Representatives.

6. There _____ a presidential election every four years.

7. There _____ two senators from each state.

8. There _____ many kinds of courts.

9. There _____ nine justices on the U.S. Supreme Court.

The Pledge of Allegiance

Sometimes, usually at meetings, we show our loyalty to the United States by saying the Pledge of Allegiance to our flag. We stand, place our right hand over our heart, and say:

I pledge allegiance to the flag
of the United States of America,
and to the republic
for which it stands,
one Nation, under God,
indivisible, with
liberty and justice for all.

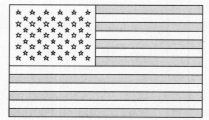

CHAPTER 10

State and Local Government

This is the capitol building in Sacramento, California.

Getting into the Reading

1. Find your state on the map of the United States in the Appendix. What are some big cities in your state? What is the state capital?

2. Look at a large map of your state. Where is the city, town, or county that you live in?

3. What government buildings are close to your home? What is each one called? Are they part of the federal government, state government, or local government? What offices or departments are located in these buildings?

Words to Know

collect	maintain	organized
contradict	National Guard	propose
issues	officials	records

State Government

State government, like the federal government, has three branches. They are the legislative branch, judicial branch, and executive branch.

The legislative branch of state government is often called the state assembly or the state legislature. Most states have a Senate and a House of Representatives. Each state decides how many senators and representatives to have and how to choose them.

The legislative branch is responsible for passing laws about state issues. It decides how much state income tax, property tax, and sales tax people should pay. Then it decides how tax money should be spent.

State legislatures also receive millions of dollars from the federal government. State governments often use federal money with state money to pay for such projects as new roads or housing for the poor.

The judicial branch of state government is the state court system. Each state has a constitution, a bill of rights, and a Supreme Court that the state courts must obey. No state law can contradict, or go against, federal law or decisions of the U.S. Supreme Court. State courts hear all cases except cases about certain federal issues.

The governor is the leader of the executive branch of state government. He or she can propose, or give ideas for, new laws to the state legislature and can veto bills she or he does not like. The governor appoints judges to state courts and is the leader of the state's National Guard. The governor also has a group of advisors. This group is much like the president's cabinet. Each advisor is responsible for one area of state government, such as education or transportation.

The lieutenant governor is the governor's assistant in the executive branch of state government. If the governor dies, the lieutenant governor becomes governor.

Your state senator and representative have offices in the state capitol and near your community. Staff members in these offices may be able to help you with state issues, such as driver's licenses, unemployment insurance, and services for the disabled.

Assembly Districts

Senate Districts

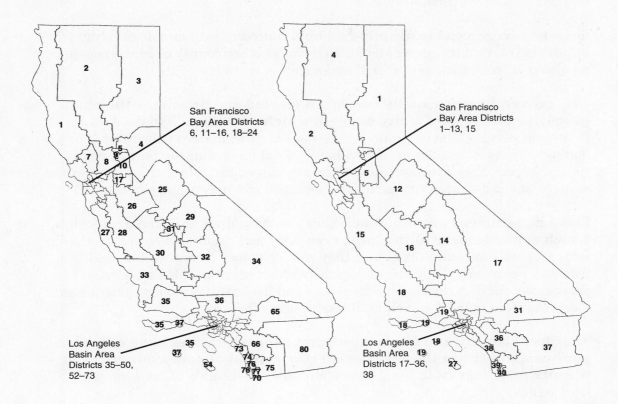

San Francisco Bay Area Districts 6, 11–16, 18–24

Los Angeles Basin Area Districts 35–50, 52–73

San Francisco Bay Area Districts 1–13, 15

Los Angeles Basin Area Districts 17–36, 38

Each state is divided into districts, or areas, that state senators and representatives take care of. Everyone's home is located in both a district served by a senator and a district served by a representative. These maps of California show how that state is divided. In California, state representative districts are based on population, so each district has about the same number of people.

Local Government

Local government includes county government and city, town, or village government. Each kind is organized, or set up, differently and each one has its own responsibilities.

County government is usually run by a board of commissioners or supervisors. County government also includes other county officials (people who hold offices), such as a sheriff and a county manager.

City government is usually run by an elected mayor, who is the chief executive officer, and a city council, which acts like a legislature. Representatives on the city council represent their own areas called wards or boroughs. Some cities, towns, and villages do not have a mayor. Sometimes in these districts, the city council hires a city manager. Still other cities, towns, and villages have an elected city commission instead of a mayor and city council.

Local government provides such services as police and fire protection, which are necessary to the local area. City and county governments charge local property and sales taxes, and they receive money from the state and federal government. They also collect money from fines people pay, such as charges for parking tickets, and from fees and licenses. Local government has a court system to handle such local issues as traffic laws.

Your local county and city government representatives have offices in your community, in the county seat (the capital of your county), or at the city or village hall. Staff members there may be able to help you with local issues.

One of local government's most important responsibilities is to manage the public schools. Local government must also provide and maintain parks and libraries; garbage collection; clean drinking water; public transportation; roads and bridges; safe streets; courthouses and jails; and marriage, birth, and death records.

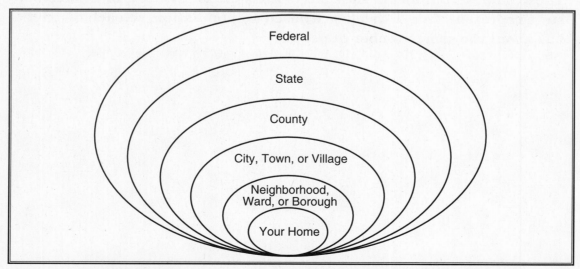

Your home is located within many levels of government.

Getting Information from the Reading

 A. Choose the best answer for each of these questions. Fill in the correct circle on the answer sheet below.

1. What is the head executive of the city government usually called?

   a. governor
   b. senator
   c. representative
   d. mayor

2. What is the head executive of the state government usually called?

   a. governor
   b. senator
   c. representative
   d. mayor

3. Which of the following is NOT an example of local government?

   a. county
   b. state
   c. city
   d. village

4. Local government does NOT

   a. run the public schools.
   b. provide police protection.
   c. issue driver's licenses.
   d. collect taxes.

Answer Sheet

1. ⓐ ⓑ ⓒ ⓓ

2. ⓐ ⓑ ⓒ ⓓ

3. ⓐ ⓑ ⓒ ⓓ

4. ⓐ ⓑ ⓒ ⓓ

These people are all local government employees.

B. Write the correct word or words in each blank to complete the sentences below. Use the words listed in the box on page 91. You may not use all of the words in the box. The first one is done for you.

1. Like the president, the governor can _____*propose*_____ new laws.

2. Your state _____ money through income, property, and sales taxes.

3. Local governments keep _____ of marriages, births, and deaths.

4. State laws cannot _____ federal laws.

5. Local governments _____ roads, bridges, and public transportation.

6. Driver's licenses, unemployment insurance, and services for the disabled are state government _____, or responsibilities.

7. The governor is the head executive of the state government and is also leader of the state's _____.

C. Answer these questions orally. Use short answers.

1. These statements are true of the federal government. Which ones are also true of state governments? Which ones are true of local governments?
    (a) It is a democratic government.
    (b) People elect their representatives.
    (c) There are three branches of government.
    (d) The government can collect taxes.
    (e) There are two houses in the legislative branch.
    (f) There is a group of people who advise the chief executive officer.
    (g) Its laws are the highest law of the land.
    (h) It controls immigration.
    (i) It can declare war.

2. Which local government services do you use? Which state government services do you use?

The N-400 Application: Parts 9, 10, 11, and 12

Everyone must fill out parts 9 and 11 of the N-400. If you are a permanent resident *and* the child of a U.S. citizen, you must fill out part 10. If you ask someone else to fill out the N-400 for you, that person must complete part 12. DO NOT FILL OUT THE LAST PART OF THE APPLICATION UNTIL THE INS EXAMINER TELLS YOU TO DO SO.

Part 9. Memberships and organizations.

A. List your present and past membership in or affiliation with every organization, association, fund, foundation, party, club, society, or similar group in the United States or in any other place. Include any military service in this part. If none, write "none". Include the name of organization, location, dates of membership and the nature of the organization. If additional space is needed, use separate paper.

_____
_____
_____
_____

Part 10. Complete only if you checked block " C " in Part 2.

How many of your parents are U.S. citizens? ☐ One   ☐ Both   (Give the following about one U.S. citizen parent:)

Family Name	Given Name	Middle Name

Address

Basis for citizenship:	Relationship to you (check one): ☐ natural parent ☐ adoptive parent
☐ Birth	
☐ Naturalization Cert. No.	☐ parent of child legitimated after birth

If adopted or legitimated after birth, give date of adoption or, legitimation: *(month/day/year)* _____

Does this parent have legal custody of you?   ☐ Yes   ☐ No

(Attach a copy of relating evidence to establish that you are the child of this U.S. citizen and evidence of this parent's citizenship.)

Part 11. Signature. *(Read the information on penalties in the instructions before completing this section).*

I certify or, if outside the United States, I swear or affirm, under penalty of perjury under the laws of the United States of America that this application, and the evidence submitted with it, is all true and correct. I authorize the release of any information from my records which the Immigration and Naturalization Service needs to determine eligibility for the benefit I am seeking.

Signature _____   Date _____

Please Note: If you do not completely fill out this form, or fail to submit required documents listed in the instructions, you may not be found eligible for naturalization and this application may be denied.

Part 12. Signature of person preparing form if other than above. *(Sign below)*

I declare that I prepared this application at the request of the above person and it is based on all information of which I have knowledge.

Signature _____   **Print Your Name** _____   Date _____

Firm Name
and Address

THE INS INTERVIEW

  A. Practice this dialogue with a partner.

INS: Are you willing to bear arms for the United States, even against your native country?

You: If I have to, yes.

INS: Okay. Here is the oath of allegiance. It says that you will give up your Mexican citizenship, that you will help protect America, and that you will be a good citizen. Sign it here and date it. You also need to sign your name on each of these pictures.

You: What is the date today?

INS: The 13th.

You: I sign my name here and where?

INS: On your photos.

INS: Here is the address where you will go for the swearing-in ceremony. Be sure to bring your green card with you.

You: Okay. Thank you very much.

  B. Now practice the dialogue with correct information about yourself.

 C. If you take the U.S. history and government test at the INS interview, you will be asked some of these questions from the INS List of 100 Questions. If you need to have the question repeated or need more time, say that.

1. What is the head executive of a state government called?

2. Who is the current governor of your state?

3. What is the capital of your state?

4. What is the head executive of a city government called?

5. Who is the head of your local government?

Interview Tip

When you go to your INS interview, you should dress as if you are going to a job interview, church, or special occasion. Wear clothes that are clean and neat. Pants or a skirt and a nice shirt or blouse are fine for women.

During the interview, make eye contact with the interviewer and relax. To Americans, this is a sign that you are telling the truth and are comfortable.

You can shake hands with the interviewer when the interview is completed.

GETTING TO KNOW ENGLISH

Future Tense

There are two ways to talk about the future in English. The first way is with a form of *be going to*. The second is with *will*.

First, use the correct present tense of the verb *be*. Then, use *going to* plus the basic verb. Examples:

You *are going to* apply for U.S. citizenship.
I *am going to* apply for U.S. citizenship.

Use *will* plus the basic verb. Examples:

You *will* apply for U.S. citizenship.
I *will* apply for U.S. citizenship.

To make a negative sentence, add the word *not*. *Won't* is the contraction, or shortened form, of *will not*. For example:

I *am not* going to be nervous.
He *will not* be nervous. You *won't* be nervous, either.

Sometimes *be going to* and *will* have different meanings. *Be going to* is used when you talk about a plan you have for the future. *Will* is used when you are willing or happy to help. For example:

After he is naturalized, he *is going to* bring his parents here from Peru.
He *will* help them learn English.

 A. Write the future tense of the verb in parentheses. Use either a form of *be going to* or *will*. The first one is done for you.

1. You (to sign) _____*are going to sign*_____ an oath of allegiance.

2. He (to need) _____ his green card at the swearing-in ceremony.

3. She (to go) _____ to the courthouse for her swearing-in ceremony.

4. The INS interviewer (to ask) _____ you some difficult questions.

5. You (to answer) _____ all of the questions correctly.

6. The INS (to check) _____ your records to be sure that everything you said is true.

7. When the interview is finished, you (to be) _____ very happy.

B. Write the future tense of the verb in parentheses. In these sentences, you can use *be going to* or *will* but not both. The first one is done for you.

1. I (to bear) _____*will bear*_____ arms for the United States.

2. I bought a new dress that I (to wear) _____ to the swearing-in ceremony.

3. If there is a war, we (to help) _____ protect America.

4. Each of us (to be) _____ a good citizen.

5. After my INS interview, I (to call) _____ my friends to tell them I did it.

6. He (to give up) _____ his Mexican citizenship.

C. Answer these questions orally.

1. What are you going to do after your INS interview?

2. What are you going to do immediately after your swearing-in ceremony?

3. As a U.S. citizen, what are your plans?

Every year, the governors of all fifty states meet.
They discuss how they can work together for
the good of their citizens.

CHAPTER 11

Making Your Voice Heard

*People vote for politicians who agree with them
and will work to support their ideas.*

Getting into the Reading

1. Many kinds of officials are elected in the United States. Which ones can you name?

2. Did you ever vote in your native country? If so, what was it like? Was it important to vote in your native country? Do you think you made a difference in the country's government when you voted?

3. Do you think it is important for U.S. citizens to vote? Why?

Words to Know

ballot	neighborhood	petition	special-interest groups
circulate	organize	protest	
endorse	participation	register	

Voting

The United States is a representative democracy. Citizens elect representatives to speak for them in the federal, state, and local government.

Voting is the most important right of U.S. citizenship. When people study the candidates, understand the issues, and think carefully about their choices, they elect high-quality representatives. The more people vote, the stronger our government is.

In the United States, all citizens who are at least 18 years old can vote. That was not always true. In the past, voters had to be 21 years old and be able to read. Men could vote but women could not. African Americans could not vote, either. Sometimes citizens even had to pay a tax in order to vote. Amendments to the Constitution and other legislation have changed all that.

Before you vote, you must register, or sign up, to vote. States have different laws about voter registration. For example, some states allow citizens to register to vote at public libraries or by mail; others have citizens register at the Board of Elections offices or the Department of Motor Vehicles. Registering to vote is a simple process and takes only a few minutes. After registering, you will receive a voter's registration card.

Next, you should study the candidates and issues. Newspapers and television provide a lot of information, as do candidate debates and other public meetings.

Special-interest groups are organizations of people who agree on certain issues. They endorse, or approve, specific candidates and explain why they think people should vote for them. There are special-interest groups for people who want to protect the environment, for those interested in women's rights, for certain religious groups, and for people who have a similar way of thinking.

When you go to vote, the election judge may ask to see a photo ID (identification) or your voter's registration card or both. The judge will give you a ballot, or sheet of paper used for voting, and show you where to go to vote. All voting is secret: no one can know how you voted. When you are finished voting, you will place your ballot in a locked box.

Voting is an important way to make your voice heard. If your neighborhood or community works together to get a candidate elected, your vote has more power. Officials work hardest for communities that vote for them in elections, and they listen carefully to the needs of people in areas with a lot of voter participation.

Other Ways to Make Your Voice Heard

In the United States, people are often successful at getting what they want from the government when they organize with other people. You can work together with people in your community or with a special-interest group.

Many communities have neighborhood organizations that work to make their area a better place to live. These organizations can ask for money to improve their neighborhood schools or for park programs. They can work with local government to fix street lights or roads. They can ask for help from the police for safer streets or bring together a group of citizens who report any unusual activity in the neighborhood.

Special-interest groups work to improve things they think are important. For example, a group of immigrants may work for more English-as-a-Second-Language classes or for a quicker naturalization process.

There are many different ways to make your voice heard.

    (a) You can call, write to, or set up a meeting with any of your public officials.

    (b) You can send a letter giving your views to your local newspaper.

    (c) You can work in the election campaign of a specific candidate.

    (d) You can sign and circulate (pass from person to person) a petition.

    (e) You can organize or attend a protest.

    (f) You can encourage people who share your ideas to vote.

    (g) You can talk about the issues with friends and neighbors.

Hundreds of mainly hispanic students in San Francisco, California, protest Proposition 187.

U.S. Senator - Our voice in Washington*   ELECTED FOR 6 YEARS

- one of two U.S. Senators who represents California's interests in Washington, D.C.
- works with U.S. Senators from other states to make new U.S. laws and votes on new laws
- as a member of Congress, helps shape the federal budget and national priorities

D E M

Dianne Feinstein

Age 61: Lives in San Francisco, CA
In my short time as U.S. Senator, I have worked hard to increase our state's federal funding by 27%, remove assault weapons form our streets, and improve our economy. I am running for a full term so I can continue to help California.

- Reduce crime by banning assault weapons and keeping violent criminals behind bars.
- Fund small business loans to create or maintain 400,000 jobs and invest in areas of the state hardest hit by the recession.
- Stop illegal immigration.

R E P

Michael Huffington

Age: 46 Lives in Santa Barbara, CA
I'm a businessman, not a career politician. I know how to create jobs for California and strengthen the economy—cut spending and keep taxes low. I do not take political action committee money. I'll represent the people of California, not the insiders and special interests.

- Safety: I'm co-chairman of "Three Strikes and Your're Out," and a lifelong death penalty supporter.
- Jobs: I voted against the Feinstein tax increase, largest in history. I favor balanced budgets, stronger defense, fewer regulations.
- End our failed welfare system.

Learning about candidates for office and their positions on issues helps voters make their decisions.

Ballot Measures*

Prop 187: Illegal Aliens. Ineligibility for Public Services

The way it is now: About 1 in 5 Californians were born in another country. Most of these 7 million people have become citizens or have official approval to be here. There are about 1.6 million illegal immigrants in California who are not authorized to be here. They are also called illegal aliens. They are not eligible for programs like welfare, but can get emergency and pre-natal health service. A child born in California to illegal immigrants is a U.S. citizen and has the same rights as other citizens.

What Prop 187 would do:
- Stop state and local agencies from providing any public education, health care or other social services to illegal immigrants except for emergency health care.
- Government agencies and schools will have to verify the legal status of anyone receiving services. They must report anyone suspected of being an illegal immigrant.
- Make it a felony to make or use a false ID that tries to get around this law.
Note: Part of Prop 187 may be overruled by a U.S. Supreme Court ruling that all children must be allowed to go to public school.

What will it cost:
- About $200 million per year would be saved from not providing health and social services to illegal immigrants.
- It could cost about $100 million to set up the systems needed to check everyone's legal status, especially for schools who have never had to check this before. After that, it might cost $10-20 million per year to verify status.
- There is a risk of losing up to $15 billion in federal funds for Medi-Cal, AFDC and education because of conflicts with federal privacy laws.

Pros:
- Prop 187 will stop the services that are attracting illegal immigrants across our border. A lot of California's population growth is because of illegal immigrants.
- We do not have enough money to provide important services to legal citizens. We cannot afford to offer services to illegal immigrants.
- The federal government is not doing a good job of stopping illegal immigration. Prop 187 takes action instead of waiting for the Feds to do something.

Cons:
- Prop 187 runs against state and federal laws and the constitution. The answer to illegal immigrations is to tighten our borders and crack down on employers who hire illegals.
- Prop 187 does not send illegal immigrants home. It will pull 400,000 students out of school and leave them on the streets.
- Prop 187 will make California a police state and increase racism. People will be suspected as illegal based on how they look and talk.

*Excerpts from *The Easy Reader Voter Guide* (November 8, 1994 General Election) developed under a grant from the California State Library to The Reading Program, Santa Clara County Library. Used with permission.

Reading the pros and cons of proposed changes to laws helps voters make informed decisions.

Getting Information from the Reading

A. Choose the best answer for each of these questions. Fill in the correct circle on the answer sheet below.

1. In addition to voting, citizens can make their voices heard by

   a. campaigning for candidates.
   b. meeting with public officials.
   c. signing or circulating a petition.
   d. all of the above

2. What is the most important right of a U.S. citizen?

   a. to attend public school
   b. to vote
   c. to carry a U.S. passport
   d. to sign a petition

3. What is the minimum voting age in the United States?

   a. 16 years
   b. 18 years
   c. 21 years
   d. 26 years

4. What are some of the ways citizens of various states can register to vote?

   a. by mail
   b. by going to the public library
   c. by going to the board of elections
   d. all of the above

Answer Sheet

1. ⓐ ⓑ ⓒ ⓓ

2. ⓐ ⓑ ⓒ ⓓ

3. ⓐ ⓑ ⓒ ⓓ

4. ⓐ ⓑ ⓒ ⓓ

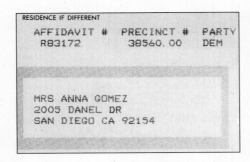

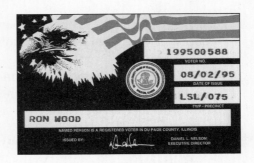

These are examples of voter's registration cards from various parts of the United States.

B. Write the correct word or words in each blank to complete the sentences below. Use the words listed in the box on page 101. You may not use all of the words in the box. The first one is done for you.

There are many opportunities for citizens to make their voices heard about legislation at the local, state, or federal level.

(a) They can _____*organize*_____ a group of people to call or write to their senator before the Senate votes.

(b) They can organize or attend a _____ against a law they think is unfair.

(c) They can circulate a _____ in their neighborhood.

(d) They can convince a special-interest group to _____ a candidate who represents their interests.

(e) They can _____ to vote and study the candidates and issues carefully.

(f) They can encourage more voter _____ from citizens in the next election.

C. Answer these questions orally. Use short answers.

1. How can you register to vote in your state?

2. Each state is divided into many small districts, called precincts, for voting. Each precinct has a specific voting, or polling, place. Where do people in your precinct go to vote?

3. State and local governments have requirements about how long you must live in your district before you can vote. What are your state and local requirements for voting?

4. Why are these things important for all citizens to do?
    Register to vote.
    Vote in all local, state, and federal elections.
    Obey the laws.
    Pay taxes every year.
    Support or protest legislation that is important to them at all levels of government.
    Serve on a jury if the court calls them.
    Volunteer to work in their neighborhood.
    Serve in the military, if called.
    Help to make their community a good place to live.
    Respect the rights of others.
    Protect their own rights.

5. Answer these questions about the following ballots from the 1992 presidential election.

OFFICIAL BALLOT (BALOTA OFICIAL)

FOR PRESIDENT (PARA PRESIDENTE	AND Y	VICE PRESIDENT VICE PRESIDENTE)		VOTE FOR ONE GROUP VOTE POR UN GRUPO	
BILL CLINTON	and (y)	AL GORE	DEMOCRATIC	55 →	●
GEORGE BUSH	and (y)	DAN QUAYLE	REPUBLICAN	56 →	○
ANDRE MARROU	and (y)	NANCY LORD	LIBERTARIAN	57 →	○
LENORA B. FULANI	and (y)	MARIA ELIZABETH MUNOZ	NEW ALLIANCE	58 →	○
JAMES MAC WARREN	and (y)	WILLIE MAE REID	SOCIALIST WORKERS	59 →	○
JAMES "BO" GRITZ	and (y)	CY MINETT	POPULIST	60 →	○
JOHN HAGELIN	and (y)	MIKE TOMPKINS	NATURAL LAW	61 →	○
ROSS PEROT	and (y)	JAMES B. STOCKDALE	INDEPENDENT	62 →	○

(a) How many presidential candidates were there in 1992?

(b) How many political parties did they represent?

(c) Can you vote for more than one candidate?

(d) Can you vote for a presidential candidate but not for a vice presidential candidate?

(e) For whom did this person vote?

(f) Who won that election?

OFFICIAL BALLOT (BALOTA OFICIAL)

FOR MAYOR PARA ALCALDE			(VOTE FOR ONE) (VOTE POR UNO)	
RAYMOND WARDINGLEY	REPUBLICAN PARTY	PARTIDO REPUBLICANO	28 →	○
RICHARD M. DALEY	DEMOCRATIC PARTY	PARTIDO DEMOCRATA	29 →	●
LAWRENCE C. REDMOND	HAROLD WASHINGTON PARTY	PARTIDO HAROLD WASHINGTON	30 →	○
ROLAND W. BURRIS	INDEPENDENT	INDEPENDIENTE	31 →	○
FOR CITY CLERK PARA SECRETARIO DE LA CIUDAD			(VOTE FOR ONE) (VOTE POR UNO)	
EDWARD G. HOWLETT	REPUBLICAN PARTY	PARTIDO REPUBLICANO	33 →	○
JAMES J. LASKI, JR.	DEMOCRATIC PARTY	PARTIDO DEMOCRATA	34 →	●
ARACELY MUNOZ	HAROLD WASHINGTON PARTY	PARTIDO HAROLD WASHINGTON	35 →	○
FOR CITY TREASURER PARA TESORERO DE LA CIUDAD			(VOTE FOR ONE) (VOTE POR UNO)	
PATRICIA ROGERS	REPUBLICAN PARTY	PARTIDO REPUBLICANO	37 →	○
MIRIAM SANTOS	DEMOCRATIC PARTY	PARTIDO DEMOCRATA	38 →	○
ARLEATHER BRANCH	HAROLD WASHINGTON PARTY	PARTIDO HAROLD WASHINGTON	39 →	○

(g) Which officials were being elected in this election?

(h) What are the responsibilities of these officials? If you do not know, how can you find out?

The Swearing-In Ceremony

Before the Ceremony

The last step in the naturalization process is the hearing or swearing-in ceremony. You will get a piece of paper with the date, time, and location for your swearing-in either at the end of your INS interview or in the mail after your interview. The paper will also give you ideas about what to wear to the ceremony.

You should arrive on time with your green card and your completed Notice of Naturalization Oath Ceremony (the N-445). You will need to talk with an INS worker to turn in your papers.

At the Ceremony

The people at the ceremony might include the judge, the court clerk (a court worker), INS workers, candidates for naturalization, and families of the candidates. Here is an abbreviated version of what might happen at a typical swearing-in ceremony.

INS Worker:	May I have your green card and N-445?
Candidate:	Sure. Here they are.
INS Worker:	Have there been any changes since you gave us your N-400?
Candidate:	No.
INS Worker:	OK. Thank you. Please find a seat in the front. Your family can sit over there.
Court Clerk:	The ceremony will begin in a moment. Please stand up. (The clerk bangs the gavel.) This court is now in session.
	(The judge comes in and sits.) (Everyone sits.)
INS Worker:	There are 235 people who are applying for naturalization here. They all meet the requirements. I recommend that the oath be given so that they can become citizens.

The Judge:	Will the candidates please stand while I read the oath? (The judge reads the entire oath.) Say "I do" and you will become U.S. citizens.

Candidates:	I do.
The Judge:	Now shake hands. You are now in this together as U.S. citizens!
	(The candidates shake hands. Families applaud.)
The Judge:	Congratulations! This day is important for you but also for our country. This nation was founded by immigrants and is based on the rights of individuals. It is your responsibility to vote and to be informed citizens. Do not give up your past and your heritage. Make it a part of our nation. This country is now your country. I congratulate each one of you and wish you happiness. God bless you. God bless America.
Court Clerk:	All rise. (The clerk bangs the gavel.) This court is adjourned. When I say your name, please come and get your certificate. **If there is a mistake on it, please tell us before you leave today.**

After the Ceremony

Now that you are a citizen, there are several things you should do.

(a) Register to vote.

(b) File petitions to bring family members to the United States.

(c) Upgrade, or bring up to date, any petitions you filed with the INS before you were a citizen. Now the INS will process them faster. Upgrading these requests will help your family come to the United States more quickly.

(d) Apply for a U.S. passport. Then, you can carry it with you when you travel. If you lose your passport, it is easier to replace than a naturalization certificate.

Keep your naturalization certificate in a safe place, such as a safe-deposit box. Do not fold your certificate because it will become difficult to read. Carry your certificate only when you need it. You can use the certificate when you travel to Mexico and Canada, countries that do not require passports from U.S. citizens, although a U.S. passport is more convenient.

Do not copy your naturalization certificate! You are permitted to copy your certificate for three purposes only:

(a) to give to the INS when you petition to bring relatives to the United States,

(b) to apply for a job that requires proof of citizenship, or

(c) to apply for your U.S. passport.

CHAPTER 12

REVIEW ACTIVITIES:
U.S. History and Government

 A. Draw a picture of the U.S. flag and label its colors.

    a. What do each of the 50 stars represent? _____

    _____

    b. What do the 13 stripes represent? _____

    _____

    c. What are the colors of the U.S. flag? _____

    _____

 B. On the map of the United States below, mark and label the following places:
    a. the thirteen original states
    b. the 49th and 50th states
    c. the capital of the United States
    d. your state and its capital
    e. the town where you live.

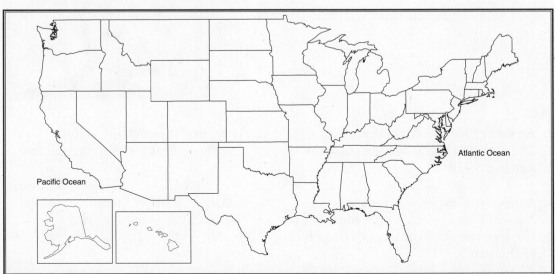

C. Work with a partner. You are Partner A. Write the answers to questions 1, 3, 5, and 7 below while Partner B writes the answers to questions 2, 4, 6, and 8 on the next page. Then, ask your partner to help you answer the questions you do not know.

1. Who is this man? _____

   What important thing did he do?

   _____

   What year did he do it? _____

3. Who are these people? _____

   Why did they come to America?

   _____

   What year did they come? _____

5. Who said, "Give me liberty or give me death"?

   _____

   When did he say this?

   _____

7. Who is this man? _____

   What was he and what important thing did he do?

   _____

   _____

2. **Answer:** Native Americans
   They helped the Pilgrims get food.
   Around 1620

4. **Answer:** George Washington
   He was the first U.S. president.
   He was the first commander-in-chief of the army.

6. **Answer:** Thomas Jefferson
   The Declaration of Independence

8. **Answer:** Martin Luther King, Jr.
   He fought for civil rights.
   In the 1960s

C. Work with a partner. You are Partner B. Write the answers to questions 2, 4, 6, and 8 below while Partner A writes the answers to questions 1, 3, 5, and 7 on the previous page. Then, ask your partner to help you answer the questions you do not know.

2. Who are these people? _____

   What important thing did they do?

   _____

   What year did they do it? _____

4. Who is this man? _____

   What was he?

   _____

   _____

6. Who is this man? _____

   What important thing did he write?

   _____

8. Who is this man?

   What important thing did he do?

   _____

   When did he do it? _____

1. **Answer:** Christopher Columbus
   He discovered America for the
   Spanish. Around 1492

3. **Answer:** Pilgrims
   For religious freedom.
   In 1620

5. **Answer:** Patrick Henry
   Before the Revolutionary War

7. **Answer:** Abraham Lincoln
   He was president during the civil
   War. He signed the Emancipation
   Proclamation to free the slaves.

D. These are important events in U.S. history. Match each event with the date it happened by drawing a line between them. The first one is done for you.

1. World War I was fought.   **a.** 1789

2. The first permanent English colony was founded in Jamestown.   **b.** 1863

3. The Declaration of Independence was adopted.   **c.** 1959

4. Christopher Columbus discovered America for Spain.   **d.** 1914 to 1918

5. The Civil War was fought.   **e.** 1964 to 1975

6. The Korean War was fought.   **f.** 1620

7. Alaska and Hawaii became the 49th and 50th states.   **g.** 1492

8. The Emancipation Proclamation was signed.   **h.** 1929 to 1939

9. The Great Depression happened.   **i.** 1920

10. The Revolutionary War was fought.   **j.** 1939 to 1945

11. The Cold War happened.   **k.** 1775 to 1783

12. The Constitution was adopted.   **l.** 1950 to 1953

13. The Vietnam War was fought.   **m.** 1776

14. World War II was fought.   **n.** 1861 to 1865

15. Women won the right to vote.   **o.** 1945 to 1991

E. Which of the government services listed below are federal government responsibilities? Which are state government responsibilities? Which are local government responsibilites? Some services may be the responsibility of more than one type of government. In that case you may use more than one letter. Write an "F" for federal, "S" for state, or "L" for local. The first one is done for you.

a. __*F*__ immigration

b. _____ road speed limits

c. _____ the voting age

d. _____ income tax

e. _____ drivers' licenses

f. _____ fishing licenses

g. _____ sales tax

h. _____ garbage pick-up

i. _____ divorce laws

j. _____ the military

k. _____ the drinking age

l. _____ police and fire departments

m. _____ mail delivery

n. _____ the library

o. _____ birth certificates

p. _____ the navy

q. _____ Social Security

r. _____ the courts

s. _____ public schools

t. _____ the lottery

u. _____ health care for poor people

F. Now look in your local phone book or at the example of telephone listings below. Find the phone number for as many of the services above as you can.

GRAFTON VILLAGE OF —
Community Activities Dept—
    1665 7th Av Grftn—
    Park-Recreation Grftn Wis 375-5310
Fire Dept-1431 13th Av Grftn —
    Emergency Grftn Wis 911
Library-USS Liberty Mem Pub Lib
    1620 11th Av Grftn 375-5315
Police Dept-1981 Wash Grftn—
    Emergency 911
Public Schools-------See Schools - Grafton Public
Public Works Dept 1300 Hickory Grftn . . 375-5325
OZAUKEE COUNTY OF —
Ciruit Court —
Branch 1
    1201 S Spring Pt Wash-**Thnsvl Tel No**   238-8357
County Clerk
    121 W Main Pt Wash----**Thnsvl Tel No**   238-8110
Sheriff—
    Emergency 911

US GOVERNMENT OF —
Health & Human Services-Dept of
Social Security Administration —
    712 Park Av W Bnd. 338-6182
Navy Recruiting Station
    1622 S Main W Bnd 338-1166
Postal Service-US —
    Grafton 1817 Highland Dr Cdrgrg 377-1990

WIS STATE OF —
Corrections Dept of —
    Community Corrections Office
        W53 N588 Higland Dr Cdrbrg 375-7940
Revenue Dept Of —
    Income and Sales Tax
        1930 Wis Av Grftn 377-6700

G. Fill in the missing information in the boxes on this chart and the chart on the next page.

FEDERAL GOVERNMENT

	Executive Branch	Legislative Branch		Judicial Branch
Title	President (Vice President) (Cabinet)	Senator	Repre-sentative	Justice of the Supreme Court
Job	To sign new bills into law, to enforce laws			
How many there are	1	100 (two from each state)		
How they are chosen	Elected by the electoral college		Election	
Name(s) of the current one(s)	1993–1997 William (Bill) Clinton (Al Gore) 1997–2001			William Rehnquist, Stephen Breyer, Ruth Bader Ginsburg, Anthony Kennedy, Sandra Day O'Connor Antonin Scalia, David Souter, John Paul Stevens, Clarence Thomas
Name for leader of the group	———			
Term of office	4 years			
Maximum number of terms	2			No limit
Where they work	White House			

| | STATE GOVERNMENT | | | LOCAL GOVERNMENT | | |
| | | | | City* | | County* |
	Executive Branch	Legislative Branch	Judicial Branch	Executive Branch	Legislative Branch	Governing Board
Title	Governor (Lieutenant Governor)	Assembly-person, Senator, Represen-tative	State Supreme Court Justice	Mayor or City Manager	City Council	Board of Commis-sioners or Supervisors
Job	To sign new bills into law				Varies by city	Varies by county
How many there are	1	Varies by state	Varies by state		Varies by city	Varies by county
How they are chosen	Election	Election	Varies by state	Elected or appointed	Varies by city	Varies by county

* City and county governments vary greatly from state to state.

✎ ETS Practice Examination

Instructions: Read each question. Pick the one best answer. Fill in the circle corresponding to the letter (A, B, C, or D) of the correct answer.

Example:

The colors of the United States flag are red, white, and

A. green.
B. orange.
C. blue.
D. brown.

The following are questions typical of those on the English and Citizenship Test. The correct answers are found on page 120.

1. Where were the 13 original American colonies?
   A In the Northwest
   B In the Southwest
   C On the West Coast
   D On the East Coast

2. The president of the United States is elected every
   A year.
   B two years.
   C three years.
   D four years.

3. The first 10 amendments to the United States Constitution are called the
   A Rights of Man.
   B Monroe Doctrine.
   C Bill of Rights.
   D Declaration of Independence.

4. Dr. Martin Luther King was a
   A civil rights leader.
   B government official.
   C college president.
   D medical scientist.

5. A mayor is the head of the government in a
   A state.
   B county.
   C city.
   D ward.

6. The first president of the United States was
   A George Washington.
   B Abraham Lincoln.
   C James Monroe.
   D John Adams.

7. The capital of the United States is
   A New York City, New York.
   B Philadelphia, Pennsylvania.
   C Washington, District of Columbia (D.C.).
   D Boston, Massachusetts.

8. Who was president of the United States during the Civil War?
   A Andrew Jackson
   B Ulysses S. Grant
   C Theodore Roosevelt
   D Abraham Lincoln

9. In 1920, an amendment to the Constitution gave women the right to.
   A hold public office.
   B own property.
   C free speech.
   D vote.

10. The judicial branch of the United States government is made up of the
    A Army and Navy.
    B State Department and Defense Department.
    C President's Cabinet.
    D Supreme Court and other federal courts.

---

1 ⒶⒷⒸⒹ	3 ⒶⒷⒸⒹ	5 ⒶⒷⒸⒹ	7 ⒶⒷⒸⒹ	9 ⒶⒷⒸⒹ
2 ⒶⒷⒸⒹ	4 ⒶⒷⒸⒹ	6 ⒶⒷⒸⒹ	8 ⒶⒷⒸⒹ	10 ⒶⒷⒸⒹ

WRITING EXERCISE: Write sentences on lines below.

_____

_____

BASIC CITIZENSHIP SKILLS PRACTICE EXAMINATION

Classroom
Version A

WRITING TEST DIRECTIONS: Your teacher will read two sentences. Write them on the lines below.

A. _____

B. _____

MULTIPLE CHOICE TEST DIRECTIONS: Read each sentence. Select the one best answer to complete each sentence. Fill in the circle for each test item in the answer box on the left.

PRACTICE ⬤ⒷⒸⒹ

1 ⒶⒷⒸⒹ
2 ⒶⒷⒸⒹ
3 ⒶⒷⒸⒹ
4 ⒶⒷⒸⒹ
5 ⒶⒷⒸⒹ
6 ⒶⒷⒸⒹ
7 ⒶⒷⒸⒹ
8 ⒶⒷⒸⒹ
9 ⒶⒷⒸⒹ
10 ⒶⒷⒸⒹ
11 ⒶⒷⒸⒹ
12 ⒶⒷⒸⒹ
13 ⒶⒷⒸⒹ
14 ⒶⒷⒸⒹ
15 ⒶⒷⒸⒹ

SCORE
Items 1-15 Writing
A Ⓞ①
B Ⓞ①
Ⓞ PASS
Ⓞ FAIL

PRACTICE

The first president of the United States was . . .
A. George Washington
B. Benjamin Franklin
C. Thomas Jefferson
D. Abraham Lincoln

1. Independence Day is on . . . .
A. January 1
B. April 15
C. July 4
D. December 25

2. There are two senators from each . . . .
A. city
B. county
C. district
D. state

3. Congress is made up of . . . .
A. the Senate and the House of Representatives
B. the president and his Cabinet
C. the Supreme Court
D. the White House

4. To vote in the United States, you must be at least . . . .
A. 16 years old
B. 18 years old
C. 21 years old
D. 25 years old

5. We elect a president every . . . .
A. two years
B. four years
C. six years
D. eight years

6. The U.S. president selects . . . .
A. the representatives
B. the governors
C. the senators
D. the Supreme Court justices

7. The head executive of a state is called . . . .
A. a governor
B. a mayor
C. a senator
D. a representative

8. A change to the U.S. Constitution is called . . . .
A. a supreme law
B. a bill
C. an amendment
D. an inauguration

9. The stripes on the U.S. flag represent the 13 original . . . .
A. states
B. amendments
C. senators
D. settlers

10. "The Star-Spangled Banner" is . . .
A. the Bill of Rights
B. the national anthem
C. the supreme law of the land
D. the introduction to the Constitution

11. The 50th state to join the United States was . . . .
A. Texas
B. Oregon
C. Hawaii
D. Idaho

12. When the Pilgrims came to America, they were helped by . . . .
A. the government
B. England
C. the president
D. the Indians

13. The Declaration of Independence was signed . . . .
A. in 1767
B. in 1776
C. in 1778
D. in 1787

14. Abraham Lincoln was president during . . .
A. the Revolutionary War
B. the Boston Tea Party
C. the Civil War
D. the War of 1812

15. Dr. Martin Luther King, Jr. was a famous . . . .
A. civil rights leader
B. senator
C. chief justice
D. governor

© CASAS

ETS Practice Examination (with Answers)

Instructions: Read each question. Pick the one best answer. Fill in the circle corresponding to the letter (A, B, C, or D) of the correct answer.

Example:

The colors of the United States flag are red, white, and
A. green.
B. orange.
C. blue.
D. brown.

The following are questions typical of those on the English and Citizenship Test. The correct answers are found on page 120.

1. Where were the 13 original American colonies?
   A In the Northwest
   B In the Southwest
   C On the West Coast
   D On the East Coast

2. The president of the United States is elected every
   A year.
   B two years.
   C three years.
   D four years.

3. The first 10 amendments to the United States Constitution are called the
   A Rights of Man.
   B Monroe Doctrine.
   C Bill of Rights.
   D Declaration of Independence.

4. Dr. Martin Luther King was a
   A civil rights leader.
   B government official.
   C college president.
   D medical scientist.

5. A mayor is the head of the government in a
   A state.
   B county.
   C city.
   D ward.

6. The first president of the United States was
   A George Washington.
   B Abraham Lincoln.
   C James Monroe.
   D John Adams.

7. The capital of the United States is
   A New York City, New York.
   B Philadelphia, Pennsylvania.
   C Washington, District of Columbia (D.C.).
   D Boston, Massachusetts.

8. Who was president of the United States during the Civil War?
   A Andrew Jackson
   B Ulysses S. Grant
   C Theodore Roosevelt
   D Abraham Lincoln

9. In 1920, an amendment to the Constitution gave women the right to
   A hold public office.
   B own property.
   C free speech.
   D vote.

10. The judicial branch of the United States government is made up of the
    A Army and Navy.
    B State Department and Defense Department.
    C President's Cabinet.
    D Supreme Court and other federal courts.

WRITING EXERCISE: Write sentences on the lines below.

There are nine justices on the Supreme Court.

George Washington was the first president of the United States.

BASIC CITIZENSHIP SKILLS PRACTICE EXAMINATION (with Answers)

DIRECTIONS: Read each sentence. Select the one best answer to complete each sentence. Fill in the circle for each question in the box on the left. When you are finished, check your answers (see back).

ANSWER KEY

PRACTICE Ⓐ Ⓑ ● Ⓓ

1. Ⓐ Ⓑ ● Ⓓ
2. Ⓐ Ⓑ ● Ⓓ
3. Ⓐ Ⓑ ● Ⓓ
4. Ⓐ ● Ⓒ Ⓓ
5. ● Ⓑ Ⓒ Ⓓ
6. Ⓐ ● Ⓒ Ⓓ
7. ● Ⓑ Ⓒ Ⓓ
8. Ⓐ ● Ⓒ Ⓓ
9. Ⓐ ● Ⓒ Ⓓ
10. Ⓐ ● Ⓒ Ⓓ
11. Ⓐ ● Ⓒ Ⓓ
12. Ⓐ ● Ⓒ Ⓓ
13. Ⓐ ● Ⓒ Ⓓ
14. Ⓐ ● Ⓒ Ⓓ
15. Ⓐ ● Ⓒ Ⓓ

PRACTICE

The first president of the United States was . . . .
A. George Washington
B. Benjamin Franklin
C. Thomas Jefferson
D. Abraham Lincoln

---

1. Independence Day is on . . . .
A. January 1
B. April 15
C. six years
D. December 25

2. There are two senators from each . . . .
A. city
B. county
C. district
D. state

3. Congress is made up of . . . .
A. the Senate and the House of Representatives
B. the president and his Cabinet
C. the Supreme Court
D. the White House

4. To vote in the United States, you must be at least . . . .
A. 16 years old
B. 18 years old
C. 21 years old
D. 25 years old

5. We elect a president every . . . .
A. two years
B. four years
C. six years
D. eight years

6. The U.S. president selects . . . .
A. the representatives
B. the governors
C. the senators
D. the Supreme Court justices

7. The head executive of a state is called . . . .
A. a governor
B. a mayor
C. a senator
D. a representative

8. A change to the U.S. Constitution is called . . . .
A. a supreme law
B. a bill
C. an amendment
D. an inauguration

9. The stripes on the U.S. flag represent the 13 original . . . .
A. states
B. amendments
C. senators
D. settlers

10. "The Star-Spangled Banner" is . . . .
A. the Bill of Rights
B. the national anthem
C. the supreme law of the land
D. the introduction to the Constitution

11. The 50th state to join the United States was . . . .
A. Texas
B. Oregon
C. Hawaii
D. Idaho

12. When the Pilgrims came to America, they were helped by . . . .
A. the government
B. England
C. the president
D. the Indians

13. The Declaration of Independence was signed . . . .
A. in 1767
B. in 1776
C. in 1778
D. in 1787

14. Abraham Lincoln was president during . . . .
A. the Revolutionary War
B. the Boston Tea Party
C. the Civil War
D. the War of 1812

15. Dr. Martin Luther King, Jr. was a famous . . . .
A. civil rights leader
B. senator
C. chief justice
D. governor

WRITING

1. _____ You must be a United States citizen to vote. _____

2. _____ Thanksgiving is a national holiday. _____

SCORING

Scoring the Writing Test:

0 points - Nothing written, not understandable, many major errors, wrote the wrong sentence, or completely illegible

1 point - Correct meaning is communicated. May contain minor grammar, spelling or capitalization errors.

To pass the test:
Minimum 9 correct out of items 1-15 and at least one of two written sentences with score of 1.

Review Activities 121

THE COMPLETE INS INTERVIEW

Practice this dialogue with a partner. Take turns being the INS interviewer. You can add questions if you want more information about something. When *you* are being interviewed, answer the questions with real information about yourself. If you do not understand the question or need more time, say that.

INS: Please remain standing and raise your right hand. Do you promise to tell the truth and nothing but the truth, so help you God?

You:

INS: Do you know what an oath is?

You:

INS: Now can I see your resident alien card, your passport, and any other identification you brought with you today?

You:

INS: Why do you want to be an American citizen?

You:

INS: Okay. We're going to go over your application to see if there have been any changes. Do you still live at the same address?

You:

INS: What was your port of entry?

You:

INS: Are you currently married?

You:

INS: How many children do you have?

You:

INS: How many times have you been absent from the United States since you got your permanent residency?

You:

INS: How long were you gone?

You:

INS: Have you ever been deported by Immigration?

You:

INS: Have you ever been arrested?

You:

INS: Do you pay your taxes every year?

You:

INS: Would you help protect America?

You:

INS: I'm going to ask you a few questions about U.S. history and government. How many states are there in the United States?

You:

INS: Name one benefit of being a citizen of the United States.

You:

INS: What is the Constitution?

You:

INS: Why do we celebrate the 4th of July?

You:

INS: What is the Bill of Rights?

You:

INS: Name three rights or freedoms guaranteed by the Bill of Rights.

You:

INS: What is the minimum voting age in the United States?

You:

INS: Name one amendment that guarantees or addresses voting rights.

You:

INS: Who makes the federal laws in the United States?

You:

INS: What is the White House?

You:

INS: Where does Congress meet?

You:

INS: What is the highest court in the United States?

You:

INS: Where does freedom of speech come from?

You:

INS: How many senators are there in Congress?

You:

INS: Good. Now I want you to write a sentence here. "My children go to school every day."

You:

INS: Good. Now I want you to sign your name here and on the margins on the photographs. Then, I want you to read this oath. It says that you will give up your Mexican citizenship, help protect America, and be a good citizen. Sign your name at the bottom.

You:

INS: You will get a letter in the mail about your swearing-in ceremony. Be sure to bring your green card with you.

You:

CHAPTER 1
Getting Information from the Reading
A. 1. d 2. d 3. b 4. b 5. a 6. a
B. 1. petition 2. naturalization
3. permanent resident 4. deported
5. truth 6. INS interview
7. allegiance 8. swearing-in
ceremony

The INS Interview
C. 1. I live in the United States of America. 2. I want to be an American citizen. 3. You must be a United States citizen to vote.
4. All citizens can vote. 5. I want to be a citizen of the United States of America.

Getting to Know English: Information Questions
A. 1. d 2. b 3. f 4. c 5. a 6. e
C. 1. What 2. When 3. Where
4. Why 5. When 6. Why
7. When 8. How 9. Who
10. What 11. When 12. Why
13. Where 14. How

CHAPTER 2
Getting Information from the Reading
A. 1. b 2. c 3. b 4. b 5. a 6. b
B. 1. Spices 2. crops 3. Silk
4. sailors 5. colonists 6. Discover
7. settle 8. reach

The INS Interview
C. 1. for religious freedom.
2. the American Indians, or Native Americans. 3. the *Mayflower*.
4. Thanksgiving. 5. the right to vote.

Getting to Know English: The Verb *Be*
A. 1. is 2. are 3. is 4. was 5. are
B. 1. was 2. was 3. were 4. was
5. were

CHAPTER 3
Getting Information from the Reading
A. 1. b 2. d 3. a 4. c 5. c 6. c 7. b
B. 1. obey 2. goods 3. commander-in-chief 4. representation 5. tax
6. pursuit 7. battles

The INS Interview
Dictation Tip
George Washington was the first president of the United States.

C. 1. George Washington was the first president. 2. July 4 is Independence Day. 3. The United States flag is red, white, and blue.
4. The American flag has thirteen (13) stripes. 5. The American flag has fifty (50) stars.

Getting to Know English: Yes/No Questions and Short Answers
A. 1. Yes, I am. No, I am not.
2. Yes, I am. No, I am not.
3. Yes, she is. No, she is not (isn't).
4. Yes, I am. No, I am not.
5. Yes, I was. No, I was not (wasn't).
B. 1. Yes, I do. No, I do not (don't).
2. Yes, I can. No, I can not (can't).
3. Yes, I do. No, I do not (don't).
4. Yes, I did. No, I did not (didn't).
5. Yes, they do. No, they do not (don't). 6. Yes, I do. No, I do not (don't). 7. Yes, I did. No, I did not (didn't).

CHAPTER 4
Getting Information from the Reading
A. 1. c 2. c 3. a 4. b 5. c
B. 1. c 2. j 3. g 4. h 5. i 6. a
7. b 8. d 9. e

The INS Interview

C. 1. Patrick Henry. 2. England. 3. Thomas Jefferson. 4. July 4, 1776. 5. That all men are created equal. 6. July 4th. England. 7. Connecticut, New Hampshire, New York, New Jersey, Massachusetts, Pennsylvania, Delaware, Virginia, North Carolina, South Carolina, Georgia, Rhode Island, Maryland. 8. George Washington. 9. "The Star-Spangled Banner." 10. Francis Scott Key. 11. Abraham Lincoln. 12. Freed the slaves. 13. Abraham Lincoln. 14. Red, white, and blue. 15. Thirteen (13). 16. They represent the original thirteen states. 17. Fifty (50). 18. One for each state in the Union. 19. Hawaii. 20. Alaska. 21. George Washington. 22. Fifty (50). 23. Colonies.

Getting to Know English: Past Tense

A. 1. reached 2. called 3. wanted 4. ended

B. 1. stopped 2. saved 3. ended 4. expanded 5. worried 6. signed 7. joined 8. worked

C. 1. brought 2. fought 3. thought 4. hurt 5. decided 6. bought 7. became 8. was 9. left

CHAPTER 5
Getting Information from the Reading

A. 1. d 2. a 3. b 4. d 5. a 6. a

B. 1. Troops 2. atomic bombs, submarines, airplanes, tanks 3. democratic 4. communist 5. resolve 6. International

The INS Interview
Dictation Tip

Now, we're going to go over your application.

C. 1. The United States is made up of fifty (50) states. 2. I live in (your state). 3. There are fifty (50) states in the United States of America. 4. Abraham Lincoln was president during the Civil War. 5. Thanksgiving is in November.

D. 1. For countries to discuss and try to resolve world problems, to provide economic aid to many countries, and occasionally to take action. 2. United Kingdom, Canada, Australia, New Zealand, Russia, China, and France.

Getting to Know English: Past Tense Questions and Short Answers

A. 1. No, it didn't. (It began in 1914.) 2. Yes, it did. 3. No, it didn't. (It fought against Germany and Austria-Hungary.) 4. Yes, it did. 5. Yes, it did. 6. No, it didn't. (Germany invaded Poland.) 7. No, it didn't. (It joined the Allies.) 8. Yes, it did. 9. No, it didn't. (Many countries did.) 10. Yes, it did. 11. No, it didn't. (North Vietnam did.) 12. (Answers will vary.) 13. No, it didn't. (It ended in 1991.)

CHAPTER 6
Getting Information from the Reading

A. 1. branch 2. philosophy 3. supreme 4. ratified 5. checks and balances

Getting Information from the Reading

A. 1. crime 2. warrant 3. print, broadcast 4. tried 5. jury 6. trial, testify 7. force 8. fine, punishment 9. guaranteed

C. 1. a 2. c 3. c 4. d 5. b 6. c 7. c

The INS Interview

D. 1. The Constitution.   2. The Preamble.   3. In 1787.   4. Three. Executive, legislative, and judicial. 5. Yes. An amendment. 6. Twenty-seven (27).   7. The Bill of Rights.   8. Everyone living in the United States.   9. Freedom of speech, press, religion, peaceable assembly, and requesting change of the government.   10. A civil rights leader.

Getting to Know English: Tag Questions

A. 1. Yes, I am. No, I'm not. 2. Yes, it was. No, it was not (wasn't). 3. Yes, I have. No, I have not (haven't). 4. Yes, I have. No, I have not (haven't).

B. 1. Yes, they can. Amendment 2. 2. Yes, they can. Amendment 6. 3. No, they can't. Amendment 4. 4. No, they can't. Amendment 5. 5. No, it isn't. Amendment 8. 6. Yes, you can. Amendment 1. 7. Yes, they are. Amendment 1. 8. No, they can't. Amendment 5. 9. No, they can't. Amendment 13. 10. No, you don't. Amendment 26.

CHAPTER 7
Getting Information from the Reading

A. 1. b 2. c 3. d 4. a 5. d 6. b 7. d
B. 1. elects 2. nominate 3. enforce, veto 4. advise, responsibilities 5. Democratic, Republican 6. requirement 7. term of office

The INS Interview

C. 1. The vice president works in Washington, D.C.   2. The White House is in Washington, D.C. 3. The president lives in the White House.   4. Washington, D.C., is the capital of the United States. 5. The president of the United States is (name of the current president).   6. There are three branches of government. 7. We have freedom of speech in the United States.   8. We are all equal in America.

E. 1. The president, vice president, cabinet, and cabinet departments. 2. (Name of current president.) 3. (Name of current vice president.) 4. The White House. 5. Washington, D.C. (1600 Pennsylvania Avenue, N.W.) 6. The electoral college.   7. Four years.   8. Two.   9. November. 10. January.   11. (Answers will vary.) Must be a U.S.-born citizen, must be at least 35 years old by the time she or he will serve, and must have lived in the United States for at least 14 years. 12. The vice president.   13. The president.   14. The cabinet. 15. The president.   George Washington.

Getting to Know English: *Can, Should, Had Better, Must,* and *Have To*

A. 1. can 2. must/have to 3. should/had better   4. should/had better 5. must/has to   6. can
B. 1. Answers will vary but may include: your name, your moral character, arrests, deportations, number of children you have. 2. Answers will vary but may include: own guns, say what we believe, practice any religion, have a lawyer, have a trial by jury. 3. Answers will vary but may include: lie to the INS, be a member of the Communist or Nazi Party, get married just to get your permanent residence, not pay your taxes, commit certain crimes, intentionally fail to register with the Selective Service.

CHAPTER 8
Getting Information from the Reading

A. 1. a 2. c 3. d 4. a 5. c 6. a 7. d

B. district, a bill (legislation), committee, debate, majority, pass, veto

The INS Interview

C. 1. Congress has two houses. 2. Congress makes the laws in the United States. 3. The House of Representatives meets in the Capitol. 4. There are two senators from each state. 5. Only Congress can declare war.

D. 1. Congress. 2. The Senate and the House of Representatives. 3. The building where Congress meets. 4. To make laws. 5. Congress. 6. The people. 7. There are two from each state. 8. Six years. 9. There is no limit. 10. (Names of the current senators from your state.) 11. 435. 12. Two years. There is no limit. 13. The Speaker of the House of Representatives. 14. Democratic and Republican.

Getting to Know English: Articles

A. 1. the 2. an 3. (nothing) 4. The 5. a 6. (nothing), the 7. the, the 8. a

CHAPTER 9
Getting Information from the Reading

A. 1. a 2. b 3. c 4. d 5. c

B. case, interpreted, ruled, system, appeal, hear

The INS Interview

C. 1. There are nine justices on the Supreme Court. 2. The courts interpret laws. 3. I believe in the Constitution.

D. 1. The Supreme Court. 2. To interpret laws. 3. Nine (9). 4. The president. 5. (Name of the current chief justice.)

Getting to Know English: *There Is/There Are*

A. 1. are 2. are 3. are 4. is 5. are 6. is 7. are 8. are 9. are

CHAPTER 10
Getting Information from the Reading

A. 1. d 2. a 3. b 4. c

B. 1. propose 2. collects 3. records 4. contradict 5. maintain 6. issues 7. National Guard

The INS Interview

C. 1. Governor. 2. (Name of the current governor.) 3. (Name of your state capital.) 4. Mayor. 5. (Name of the current leader of local government.)

Getting to Know English: Future Tense

A. 1. are going to sign/will sign 2. is going to need/will need 3. is going to go/will go 4. is going to ask/will ask 5. are going to answer/will answer 6. is going to check/will check 7. are going to be/will be

B. 1. will bear 2. am going to wear/will wear 3. will help/are going to help 4. will be/is going to be 5. will call/am going to call 6. will give up/is going to give up

CHAPTER 11
Getting Information from the Reading

A. 1. d 2. b 3. b 4. d

B. a. organize b. protest c. petition d. endorse e. register f. participation

CHAPTER 12
REVIEW ACTIVITIES: U.S. History and Government

A. Picture of U.S. flag is on page 129. a. one of the states b. the original thirteen states c. red, white, and blue

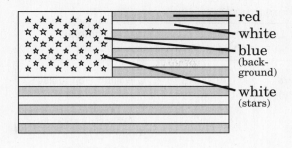

red
white
blue (background)
white (stars)

B. The answers to *a* through *c* are indicated on the map below. Answers to *d* and *e* will vary.

C. Answers to questions 1, 3, 5, and 7 appear on p. 113; answers to questions 2, 4, 6, and 8 appear on p. 112.

D. 1. d 2. f 3. m 4. g 5. n 6. l 7. c 8. b 9. h 10. k 11. o 12. a 13. e 14. j 15. i

E. a. F b. F, S, L c. F d. F, S e. S f. S g. S, L h. L i. S j. F k. S l. L m. F n. L o. L p. F q. F r. F, S, L s. L t. S u. F, S, L

F. Answers will vary.

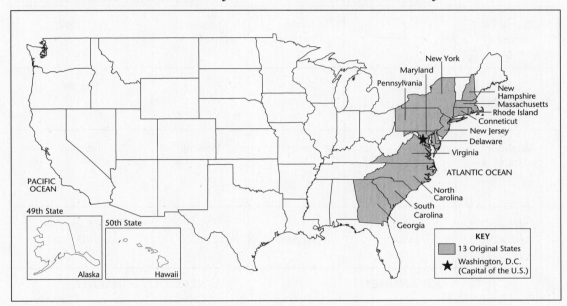

G. FEDERAL GOVERNMENT (Chapter 12, continued)

	Executive Branch	Legislative Branch		Judicial Branch
Title	President (Vice President) (Cabinet)	Senator	Representative	Justice of the Supreme Court
Job	To sign new bills into law, to enforce laws	To make laws	To make laws	To interpret laws
How many there are	1	100 (two from each state)	435	9
How they are chosen	Elected by the electoral college	Election	Election	Appointed by the president

FEDERAL GOVERNMENT (Chapter 12, continued)

	Executive Branch	Legislative Branch		Judicial Branch
Name(s) of the current one(s)	*1993–1997* William (Bill) Clinton (Al Gore) *1997–2001*	(answers will vary)	(answers will vary)	William Rehnquist, Stephen Breyer, Ruth Bader Ginsberg, Anthony Kennedy, Sandra Day O'Connor, Antonin Scalia, David Souter, John Paul Stevens, Clarence Thomas
Name for leader of the group	———	Vice President	Speaker of the House	Chief Justice
Term of office	4 years	2 years	6 years	For life
Maximum number of terms	2	No limit	No limit	No limit
Where they work	White House	The Capitol	The Capitol	The Supreme Court Building

STATE GOVERNMENT   LOCAL GOVERNMENT
                                                              City   County

Executive Branch	Legislative Branch	Judicial Branch	Executive Branch	Legislative Branch	Governing Board
Governor (Lieutenant Governor)	Assembly-person or Senator, Representative	State Supreme Court Justice	Mayor or City Manager	City Council	Board of Commissioners or Supervisors
To sign new bills into state law	To make state laws	To interpret state laws	Varies by city	Varies by city	Varies by county
1	Varies by state	Varies by state	1	Varies by city	Varies by county
Election	Election	Varies by state	Elected or appointed	Varies by city	Varies by county

CHAPTER 1
The INS Interview
B. Now practice the dialogue using correct information about yourself.

INS: Let me check some information. What is your complete name?

INS: What is your home address?

INS: May I please have your passport, resident alien card, and a photo ID? Your driver's license or state ID is fine.

INS: I need your passport, your green card, and a photo ID.

INS: Your current citizenship is?

INS: What is your citizenship now?

INS: What was your port of entry?

INS: What is your marital status?

INS: Have you been married before?

INS: Were you ever married to anyone else?

INS: Have you left the United States since you became a permanent resident?

INS: For how long?

C. During the INS interview, the interviewer will read a sentence to you. You then must write the sentence correctly in English. Practice by listening carefully and writing the sentences that you hear. The first one is done for you.

1. I live in the United States of America.
2. I want to be an American citizen.
3. You must be a United States citizen to vote.
4. All citizens can vote.
5. I want to be a citizen of the United States of America.

CHAPTER 2
The INS Interview
B: Now practice the dialogue using correct information about yourself.

INS: Please remain standing and raise your right hand. Do you promise to tell the truth and nothing but the truth, so help you God?

INS: Do you swear that all the information on your application, the documents you submitted, and the information you give today is the truth?

INS: You may sit down. Do you understand what an oath is?

INS: Right. You are here for your naturalization interview. Why do you want to be a U.S. citizen?

INS: We're going to go over your application to see if there are any changes. Do you still live at the same address?

INS: Do you still work for the same employer?

INS: How long have you worked there?

INS: Do you still have the same position?

INS: Do you still have the same job?

CHAPTER 3
The INS Interview
B. Now practice the dialogue using correct information about yourself.

INS: Now we're going to go over your application to see if there are any changes since you submitted it. Is your address still the same?

INS: You have been a permanent resident since 1985?

INS: Are you currently married?

INS: You have been absent from the United States how many times since you got your permanent residence?

INS: When?

INS: And before that?

Dictation Tip

Sometimes when we speak, we do not say every word clearly. Listen carefully to this sentence.
George Washington was the first president of the United States.
How many words did you hear?

Listen again. This time write the words you hear.
George Washington was the first president of the United States.

Look carefully at what you wrote. Which words are missing? Listen carefully again.
George Washington was the first president of the United States.
Did you hear more words? Write them.

C. During the INS interview, the interviewer will read a sentence to you. You then must write the sentence correctly in English. Practice by listening carefully and writing the sentences that you hear. The first one is done for you.

1. George Washington was the first president.
2. July 4 is Independence Day.
3. The United States flag is red, white, and blue.
4. The American flag has thirteen stripes.
5. The American flag has fifty stars.

CHAPTER 4
The INS Interview
B. Now practice the dialogue using correct information about yourself.
INS: Are you currently married?
INS: For how long have you been married?
INS: Before that?
INS: Did you marry to get your green card?

CHAPTER 5
The INS Interview
B. Now practice the dialogue using correct information about yourself.
INS: Is your name Martínez Peter?
INS: Are you sure?
INS: Do you want to change your name legally when you become a citizen?
INS: When did you get your permanent residency?
INS: Did you leave the United States in 1990 and 1994?
INS: Did you stay for more than six months?
INS: Did you get permission to return from the INS?
INS: Did you return as a permanent resident and enter with your permanent resident card?
INS: Did you originally enter the United States through New York City?
INS: When was that?

Dictation Tip

When we speak English, we do not always speak clearly. Sometimes we combine two words so that they sound like one word. Listen carefully to this sentence.
Now we're going to go over your application.
How many words did you hear?

Listen again and write down the words you hear.
Now we're going to go over your application.

Look carefully at what you wrote. Think about the beginnings and ends of the words. Is the end of one word combined with the beginning of the next word so that it sounds like one word, or like a different word? Listen carefully again. Write down the words you hear.
Now we're going to go over your application.

C. During the INS interview, the interviewer will read a sentence to you. You then must write the sentence correctly in English. Practice by listening carefully and writing the sentences that you hear. The first one is done for you.
1. The United States is made up of fifty states.
2. I live in (your state).
3. There are fifty states in the United States of America.
4. Abraham Lincoln was president during the Civil War.
5. Thanksgiving is in November.

CHAPTER 6
The INS Interview
C. Now practice the dialogue with correct information about yourself. Tell the interviewer in different ways that you do not understand the question.
INS: You were a member of the Communist Party, weren't you?
INS: Do you believe in communism?

CHAPTER 7
The INS Interview
B. Now practice the dialogue using correct information about yourself.
INS: Did you register for the Selective Service?
INS: Do you know your selective service number?
INS: Did you get the information?
INS: Do you file your tax returns every year?

C. During the INS interview, the interviewer will read a sentence to you. You then must write the sentence correctly in English. Practice by listening carefully and writing the sentences that you hear. The first one is done for you.
1. The vice president works in Washington, D.C.
2. The White House is in Washington, D.C.
3. The president lives in the White House.
4. Washington, D.C., is the capital of the United States.
5. The president of the United States is (name of the president).
6. There are three branches of government.
7. We have freedom of speech in the United States.
8. We are all equal in America.

CHAPTER 8
The INS Interview
B. Now practice the dialogue using correct information about yourself.

INS: Why are you applying for naturalization?

INS: Have you ever been deported by immigration?

INS: When?

INS: Were you deported, or did you return to your native country voluntarily?

INS: Have you ever been arrested?

INS: Any other arrests?

C. During the INS interview, the interviewer will read a sentence to you. You then must write the sentence correctly in English. Practice by listening carefully and writing the sentences that you hear.

1. Congress has two houses.
2. Congress makes the laws in the United States.
3. The House of Representatives meets in the Capitol.
4. There are two senators from each state.
5. Only Congress can declare war.

CHAPTER 9
The INS Interview
B. Now practice the dialogue using correct information about yourself.

INS: Do you know what the U.S. Constitution is?

INS: Do you believe in the Constitution and our form of government?

INS: If the government asked, would you bear arms or serve in the United States armed forces in another capacity?

C. During the INS interview, the interviewer will read a sentence to you. You then must write the sentence correctly in English. Practice by listening carefully and writing the sentences that you hear.

1. There are nine justices on the Supreme Court.
2. The courts interpret laws.
3. I believe in the Constitution.

CHAPTER 10
The INS Interview
B. Now practice the dialogue using correct information about yourself.

INS: Are you willing to bear arms for the United States, even against your native country?

INS: Okay. Here is the oath of allegiance. It says that you will give up your citizenship, that you will help protect America, and that you will be a good citizen. Sign it here and date it. You also need to sign your name on each of these pictures.

INS: Here is the address where you will go for the swearing-in ceremony. Be sure to bring your green card with you.

MAP OF THE UNITED STATES

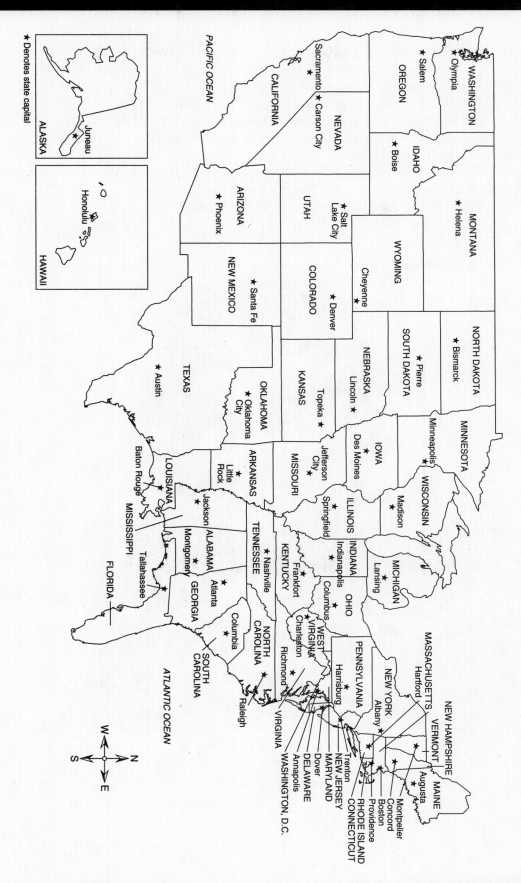

★ Denotes state capital

PACIFIC OCEAN

ALASKA
★ Juneau

HAWAII
Honolulu

WASHINGTON
★ Olympia
★ Salem
OREGON

IDAHO
★ Boise

CALIFORNIA
★ Sacramento

NEVADA
★ Carson City

MONTANA
★ Helena

WYOMING
Cheyenne ★

ARIZONA
★ Phoenix

UTAH
★ Salt Lake City

COLORADO
★ Denver

NORTH DAKOTA
★ Bismarck

SOUTH DAKOTA
★ Pierre

NEBRASKA
Lincoln ★

NEW MEXICO
★ Santa Fe

KANSAS
Topeka ★

MINNESOTA
★ Minneapolis

IOWA
Des Moines ★

WISCONSIN
★ Madison

TEXAS
★ Austin

OKLAHOMA
★ Oklahoma City

MISSOURI
Jefferson City ★

ILLINOIS
Springfield ★

INDIANA
Indianapolis ★

MICHIGAN
Lansing ★

ARKANSAS
Little Rock ★

LOUISIANA
Baton Rouge ★

MISSISSIPPI
Jackson ★

ALABAMA
Montgomery ★

TENNESSEE
Nashville ★

KENTUCKY
Frankfort ★

OHIO
Columbus ★

FLORIDA
Tallahassee ★

GEORGIA
Atlanta ★

SOUTH CAROLINA
Columbia ★

NORTH CAROLINA
Raleigh ★

WEST VIRGINIA
Charleston ★

VIRGINIA
Richmond ★

PENNSYLVANIA
Harrisburg ★

NEW YORK
Albany ★

MASSACHUSETTS
Hartford ★

NEW HAMPSHIRE
VERMONT
Montpelier
Concord

MAINE
Augusta

Boston
Providence
RHODE ISLAND
CONNECTICUT
Trenton
NEW JERSEY
Dover
DELAWARE
MARYLAND
Annapolis
WASHINGTON, D.C.

ATLANTIC OCEAN

W
S — N
E

Words by Francis Scott Key

Oh say, can you see, by the dawn's early light,
What so proudly we hailed at the twilight's last gleaming?
Whose broad stripes and bright stars, through the perilous fight,
O'er the ramparts we watched, were so gallantly streaming!
And the rockets' red glare, the bombs bursting in air,
Gave proof through the night that our flag was still there.
Oh say, does that star-spangled banner yet wave
O'er the land of the free and the home of the brave?

Francis Scott Key

1. What are the colors of our flag?
   Red, white, and blue

2. How many stars are there on our flag?
   50

3. What color are the stars on our flag?
   White

4. What do the stars on the flag mean?
   One for each state in the Union

5. How many stripes are there on the flag?
   13

6. What color are the stripes?
   Red and white

7. What do the stripes on the flag mean?
   They represent the original 13 states.

8. How many states are there in the union?
   50

9. Why do we celebrate the 4th of July?
   Independence Day

10. What is the date of Independence Day?
    July 4th

11. Independence from whom?
    England

12. What country did we fight during the Revolutionary War?
    England

13. Who was the first president of the United States?
    George Washington

14. Who is the president of the United States today?
    (Name of the current president)

15. Who is the vice president of the United States today?
    (Name of the current vice president)

16. Who elects the president of the United States?
    The electoral college

17. Who becomes president of the United States if the president should die?
    The vice president

18. For how long do we elect the president?
    Four years

19. What is the Constitution?
    The supreme law of the land

20. Can the Constitution be changed?
    Yes

21. What do we call a change to the Constitution?
    An amendment

22. How many changes or amendments are there to the Constitution?
    27

23. How many branches are there in our government?
    3

24. What are the three branches of our government?
Legislative, executive, and judiciary

25. What is the legislative branch of our government?
Congress

26. Who makes the federal laws in the United States?
Congress

27. What is Congress?
The Senate and the House of Representatives

28. What is the duty of Congress?
To make laws

29. Who elects Congress?
The people

30. How many senators are there in Congress?
100

31. Can you name the two senators from your state?
(Names of current senators from your state)

32. For how long do we elect each senator?
6 years

33. How many voting members are there in the House of Representatives?
435

34. For how long do we elect the Representatives?
2 years

35. What is the executive branch of our government?
The president, vice president, cabinet, and departments under the cabinet members

36. What is the judiciary branch of our government?
The Supreme Court

37. What are the duties of the Supreme Court?
To interpret laws

38. What is the supreme law of the United States?
The Constitution

39. What is the Bill of Rights?
The first ten amendments to the Constitution

40. What is the capital of your state?
(Name of the capital of your state)

41. Who is the current governor of your state?
(Name of the current governor of your state)

42. Who becomes president of the United States if the president and the vice president should die?
Speaker of the House of Representatives

43. Who is the Chief Justice of the Supreme Court?
William Rehnquist

44. Can you name the thirteen original colonies?
Connecticut, New Hampshire, New York, New Jersey, Massachusetts, Pennsylvania, Delaware, Virginia, North Carolina, South Carolina, Georgia, Rhode Island, and Maryland

45. Who said, "Give me liberty or give me death"?
Patrick Henry

46. Which countries were our allies during World War II?
United Kingdom, Canada, Australia, New Zealand, Russia, China, and France

47. What is the 49th state added to our Union?
Alaska

48. How many full terms can a president serve?
2

49. Who was Martin Luther King, Jr.?
A civil rights leader

50. Who is the head of your local government?
(Name of the current head of your local government)

51. According to the Constitution, a person must meet certain requirements in order to be eligible to become president. Name one of these requirements.
Must be a U.S.-born citizen of the United States; must be at least 35 years old by the time he/she will serve; must have lived in the United States for at least 14 years

52. Why are there 100 senators in the United States Senate?
2 from each state

53. Who nominates Supreme Court justices?
Nominated by the president

54. How many Supreme Court justices are there?
9

55. Why did the Pilgrims come to America?
For religious freedom

56. What is the head executive of a state government called?
Governor

57. What is the head executive of a city government called?
Mayor

58. What holiday was celebrated for the first time by the American colonists?
Thanksgiving

59. Who was the main writer of the Declaration of Independence?
Thomas Jefferson

60. When was the Declaration of Independence adopted?
July 4, 1776

61. What is the basic belief of the Declaration of Independence?
That all men are created equal

62. What is the national anthem of the United States?
"The Star-Spangled Banner"

63. Who wrote "The Star-Spangled Banner"?
Francis Scott Key

64. Where does freedom of speech come from?
The Bill of Rights

65. What is the minimum voting age in the United States?
18

66. Who signs bills into law?
The president

67. What is the highest court in the United States?
The Supreme Court

68. Who was president during the Civil War?
Abraham Lincoln

69. What did the Emancipation Proclamation do?
Freed many slaves

70. What special group advises the president?
The cabinet

71. Which president is called "the father of our country"?
George Washington

72. What is the 50th state added to our Union?
Hawaii

73. Who helped the Pilgrims in America?
The American Indians (Native Americans)

74. What is the name of the ship that brought the pilgrims to America?
The Mayflower

75. What were the 13 original states of the United States called?
Colonies

76. Name three rights or freedoms guaranteed by the Bill of Rights.
a. *The right of freedom of speech, press, religion, peaceable assembly, and requesting change of government.*
b. *The right to bear arms (the right to have lawful weapons, including firearms, though subject to certain regulations).*
c. *The government may not quarter or house soldiers in private homes during peacetime without the owner's consent.*
d. *The government may not search or take a person's property without a warrant.*
e. *A person may not be tried twice for the same crime and does not have to testify against him- or herself.*
f. *A person charged with a crime still has many rights, such as the right to a trial and to be represented by a lawyer.*
g. *The right to trial by jury in most cases.*
h. *Protects people against excessive or unreasonable fines or cruel and unusual punishment.*
i. *The people have rights other than those mentioned in the Constitution.*
j. *Any power not given to the federal government by the Constitution is a power reserved to the state or the people.*

77. Who has the power to declare war?
Congress

78. Name one amendment that guarantees or addresses voting rights.
15th, 19th, 24th, and 26th

79. Which president freed the slaves?
Abraham Lincoln

80. In what year was the Constitution written?
1787

81. **What are the first ten amendments to the Constitution called?**
The Bill of Rights

82. **Name one purpose of the United Nations.**
For countries to discuss and try to resolve world problems; to provide economic aid to many countries; occasionally to take action

83. **Where does Congress meet?**
In the Capitol, in Washington, D.C.

84. **Whose rights are guaranteed by the Constitution and the Bill of Rights?**
Everyone living in the United States

85. **What is the introduction to the Constitution called?**
The Preamble

86. **Name one benefit of being a citizen of the United States.**
Vote; travel with a U.S. passport; serve on a jury; apply for federal employment opportunities

87. **What is the most important right granted to U.S. citizens?**
The right to vote

88. **What is the United States Capitol?**
The place where Congress meets

89. **What is the White House?**
The president's official residence

90. **Where is the White House located?**
Washington, D.C. (1600 Pennsylvania Avenue, N.W.)

91. **What is the name of the president's official home?**
The White House

92. **Name one right guaranteed by the first amendment.**
Freedom of speech, press, religion, peaceable assembly, and requesting change of the government

93. **Who is the commander-in-chief of the U.S. Army and Navy?**
The president

94. **Which president was the first commander-in-chief of the U.S. Army and Navy?**
George Washington

95. **In which month do we vote for the president?**
November

96. **In which month is the new president inaugurated?**
January

97. **How many times may a senator be reelected?**
There is no limit

98. **How many times may a congressman be reelected?**
There is no limit

99. **What are the two major political parties in the United States today?**
Democratic and Republican

100. **How many states are there in the United States?**
50

TEST PROCEDURES FOR THE ETS ENGLISH AND CITIZENSHIP EXAMINATION FOR NATURALIZATION

Suggested Verbal Instructions:

We are about to begin the actual test. Please do not answer the questions out loud. Do not give help to other test takers and do not let other test takers help you. It is important that you do not create a disturbance during the test. If you do these things, you will be asked to leave and your test will not be scored.

I will read each question out loud to you as you read along in your test book. Silently and on your own, you will read the answer choices that are printed in your test book. Each question has four possible answers: the A answer, B answer, C answer, and the D answer. Read each possible answer and choose which is correct. Only one answer is correct. Mark the answers you choose in the box marked "Multiple Choice - A."

The proctor will hold up the answer sheet and point to the box.

Question number 1

Slowly and clearly, the proctor will read the test question but not the answer choices. The proctor will then pause 30 to 40 seconds to allow test takers time to read the answer choices and to mark their answers. After completing all 20 questions, the proctor says:

Please take a few minutes to check over your answers. If you change any answer, be sure to erase the answer you are changing after you mark the new answer.

After a few minutes, the proctor says:

I will now collect the test books.

Collect the books in serial order, making sure every book is returned. Then say:

It is time to do the writing exercise. This is a test of your ability to write in English. You will write the sentence that I read to you. I will read the sentences two times. In the "A"box, under the heading "Writing Exercise: Write sentence in box below," you must write the sentence carefully and neatly so it is easy to read.

Show the test takers the box. After a few minutes say:

Now, I will read the sentence to you—write it in the box.

Pause and then slowly read the sentence two times. After a few minutes, say:

Please turn your answer sheet over. Leave your photo ID on your desk. You may now stand and relax a minute or two. You do not need to stay for the second test, but you are encouraged to do so. Remember, to pass the test you must correctly answer at least 12 of the 20 questions and properly complete one writing exercise. The second test will begin in a few minutes. If you are not staying for the second test, please raise your hand and I will collect your answer sheet.

I will give you a receipt that shows you have taken the test. Be sure to fill in the information on the receipt. Today's date is _____ and the test center number is _____. Keep this information until you have received your test scores from ETS. You should receive your scores within four weeks. If you have not received your scores by _____(date), you may call ETS toll free at the number printed on your receipt.

For information on ETS test sites call 1(800)358-6230.

NEW CITIZENS PROJECT
English and Citizenship Examination for Naturalization

USE ONLY A NO. 2 PENCIL FOR COMPLETING THIS SHEET. ERASE ERRORS AND STRAY MARKS COMPLETELY.

PLEASE BE SURE EACH MARK COMPLETELY FILLS THE INTENDED CIRCLE AS ILLUSTRATED HERE: ●

SIDE 1

In the column below the box in which you have entered a letter for your name, find the circle with the same letter and fill it in completely.

1. Last Name | **First Name** | **MI**

3. Alien Registration Number

4. Test Center

SAMPLE

5. Sex (Optional)

Female ●

Male Ⓜ

6. Date of Birth (Optional)

M M D D Y Y

Mark Reflex® by NCS EM-161286:654321

2. PLEASE PRINT

Name as it is on Alien Registration Card

NAME: _____
Last Name   First Name   M. I.

Address (Be sure to include your apartment number if any)

ADDRESS: _____
Street Address   Apt. # (If any)

_____
City   State or Province   Zip Code

TELEPHONE NUMBER: ( )
Area Code

SIGNATURE: _____

7. Language
YOUR TEST IS PRINTED IN:

⓪	English
●	Chinese / Cantonese
②	Chinese / Mandarin
③	Hindi
④	Korean
⑤	Polish
⑥	Russian
⑦	Spanish
⑧	Vietnamese
⑨	Other

Practice:

1 Ⓐ ● Ⓒ Ⓓ

2 ● Ⓑ ● Ⓓ

3 Ⓐ Ⓑ Ⓒ ●

Last Name

First Name

TEST DATE

MO | DAY | YR

1 - 688 - Alien Registration Card Number

TEST CENTER

MULTIPLE CHOICE - A

IMPORTANT: Fill in the circles with the same number as the FORM NUMBER that is printed on the cover of your test book.

Form Number

1 ● Ⓑ Ⓒ Ⓓ   6 Ⓐ ● Ⓒ Ⓓ   11 Ⓐ Ⓑ Ⓒ Ⓓ   16 Ⓐ Ⓑ ● Ⓓ

2 Ⓐ ● Ⓒ Ⓓ   7 Ⓐ Ⓑ ● Ⓓ   12 Ⓐ Ⓑ ● Ⓓ   17 Ⓐ Ⓑ Ⓒ ●

3 Ⓐ Ⓑ ● Ⓓ   8 Ⓐ Ⓑ ● Ⓓ   13 Ⓐ Ⓑ Ⓒ ●   18 ● Ⓑ Ⓒ Ⓓ

4 Ⓐ Ⓑ Ⓒ ●   9 ● Ⓑ Ⓒ Ⓓ   14 Ⓐ Ⓑ Ⓒ Ⓓ   19 Ⓐ ● Ⓒ Ⓓ

5 ● Ⓑ Ⓒ Ⓓ   10 Ⓐ ● Ⓒ Ⓓ   15 ● Ⓑ Ⓒ Ⓓ   20 Ⓐ Ⓑ ● Ⓓ

WRITING EXERCISE: Write sentence in box below. Do not write outside of box.

①
②
③

MULTIPLE CHOICE - B

IMPORTANT: Fill in the circles with the same number as the FORM NUMBER that is printed on the cover of your test book.

Form Number

1 ● Ⓑ Ⓒ Ⓓ   6 Ⓐ Ⓑ ● Ⓓ   11 Ⓐ ● Ⓒ Ⓓ   16 Ⓐ Ⓑ Ⓒ ●

2 ● Ⓑ Ⓒ Ⓓ   7 Ⓐ Ⓑ Ⓒ ●   12 Ⓐ ● Ⓒ Ⓓ   17 ● Ⓑ Ⓒ Ⓓ

3 Ⓐ ● Ⓒ Ⓓ   8 Ⓐ Ⓑ ● Ⓓ   13 Ⓐ Ⓑ ● Ⓓ   18 ● Ⓑ Ⓒ Ⓓ

4 Ⓐ Ⓑ ● Ⓓ   9 Ⓐ Ⓑ ● Ⓓ   14 Ⓐ Ⓑ Ⓒ Ⓓ   19 Ⓐ ● Ⓒ Ⓓ

5 Ⓐ Ⓑ ● Ⓓ   10 Ⓐ Ⓑ Ⓒ Ⓓ   15 Ⓐ Ⓑ Ⓒ ●   20 ● Ⓑ Ⓒ Ⓓ

WRITING EXERCISE: Write sentence in box below. Do not write outside of box.

①
②
③

Suggested Verbal Instructions:

Make sure you use a No. 2 pencil.

Fill the circles completely.

If you make a mistake, make sure that the old marks are completely erased. The computer will read all darkened circles and pencil marks.

Take out your photo ID and INS card and copy your name exactly as it appears on the card. Please leave your INS card and photo ID out on the desk. Then fill out your address and the other information at the top of the answer sheet in items 1–5. Use the information written on the blackboard (or overhead transparency) to complete items 6 and 8.

Turn your answer sheet to the side and fill out your name, this test site name, and today's date. Do not write in the box that says "For Official Use Only."

Fill in #9, Registrant Status. If you paid $22 to take the test, bubble in "Pre-Registration." If you paid $26, fill in "Walk-in / Late Registrant."

If you failed the exam the first time and are taking it again, fill in "Re-take with Voucher." If you registered to take the exam before but were unable to take it, fill in "Re-schedule."

Do not open the test booklets yet.

Do not write in the test booklets.

Open your test booklets to page 1. These are practice items for the test. Find the boxes for practice items 1 and 2 on the answer sheet.

Listen to the tape and follow the directions to answer the practice items. Please don't talk during the test so everyone can hear the tape. Listen and do the best you can. Start with number 1 under "Begin Test" on your answer sheet. Please do your own work. There is no talking during the test. Are there any questions? Turn to page 2. Begin the test.

Everyone stop writing. Put your pencils down, close your test booklets, and turn your answer sheets over.

Note to Proctor: Collect and count all test booklets before giving the writing test.

Read this script aloud, clearly, and at a normal pace.

Now let's start the Writing Section of the test.

*Find letters A and B near the bottom of your answer sheet, where it says **Writing Test**.*(Hold up an answer sheet and point to the Writing Test section toward the bottom of the page. Pause 5 seconds.)

I am going to read two sentences in English. Listen and write the sentences on lines A and B near the bottom of the answer sheet. You will hear each sentence three times.

Now listen and get ready to write the sentences. Let's begin.

Sentence A.   George Bush was president of the United States.
(Pause 5 seconds.)

Sentence A.   George Bush was president of the United States.
(Pause 5 seconds.)

Sentence A.   George Bush was president of the United States.
(Pause 10 seconds.)

Sentence B.   You must be a U.S. citizen to vote.   (Pause 5 seconds.)

Sentence B.   You must be a U.S. citizen to vote.   (Pause 5 seconds.)

Sentence B.   You must be a U.S. citizen to vote.   (Pause 10 seconds.)

The test is now over. Everyone stop writing. Please review your answer sheet to make sure your marks are dark and solid. If you changed an answer, make sure the old mark is completely erased.

Proctors! Do not forget to say:

Now please sign your name near the bottom of the answer sheet, next to where it says, 'Examinee's Signature' and hand in your answer sheets.

Make sure the examinees have bubbled in Section 10 on the answer sheet (Registrant Status)!

Anyone who does not want to wait for their test results may now leave. You will receive official test results in the mail in about three weeks.

If you want your unofficial test results today, please hand in your answer sheet, leave the room, and wait until your name is called.

For information about CASAS test sites call 1(800)929-3743.

BASIC CITIZENSHIP SKILLS EXAMINATION

PRACTICE 1
Ⓐ Ⓑ Ⓒ Ⓓ

PRACTICE 2
Ⓐ Ⓑ Ⓒ Ⓓ

BEGIN TEST

1 Ⓐ Ⓑ Ⓒ Ⓓ
2 Ⓐ Ⓑ Ⓒ Ⓓ
3 Ⓐ Ⓑ Ⓒ Ⓓ
4 Ⓐ Ⓑ Ⓒ Ⓓ
5 Ⓐ Ⓑ Ⓒ Ⓓ
6 Ⓐ Ⓑ Ⓒ Ⓓ
7 Ⓐ Ⓑ Ⓒ Ⓓ
8 Ⓐ Ⓑ Ⓒ Ⓓ
9 Ⓐ Ⓑ Ⓒ Ⓓ
10 Ⓐ Ⓑ Ⓒ Ⓓ
11 Ⓐ Ⓑ Ⓒ Ⓓ
12 Ⓐ Ⓑ Ⓒ Ⓓ
13 Ⓐ Ⓑ Ⓒ Ⓓ
14 Ⓐ Ⓑ Ⓒ Ⓓ
15 Ⓐ Ⓑ Ⓒ Ⓓ
16 Ⓐ Ⓑ Ⓒ Ⓓ
17 Ⓐ Ⓑ Ⓒ Ⓓ
18 Ⓐ Ⓑ Ⓒ Ⓓ
19 Ⓐ Ⓑ Ⓒ Ⓓ
20 Ⓐ Ⓑ Ⓒ Ⓓ
21 Ⓐ Ⓑ Ⓒ Ⓓ
22 Ⓐ Ⓑ Ⓒ Ⓓ
23 Ⓐ Ⓑ Ⓒ Ⓓ
24 Ⓐ Ⓑ Ⓒ Ⓓ
25 Ⓐ Ⓑ Ⓒ Ⓓ

This information is very important. Please print clearly.

1. Name _____
PLEASE PRINT YOUR NAME AS IT APPEARS ON YOUR INS CARD

2. Address _____
MAILING ADDRESS   APT. NUMBER

CITY   STATE   ZIP

3. Birthdate ___/___/___
MONTH DAY YEAR

4. Today's Date ___/___/___
MONTH DAY YEAR

5. Telephone Number (___ ___ ___) ___ ___ ___ — ___ ___ ___ ___
AREA CODE

6. Agency I.D.   Site I.D.   7. Write your INS Number Here   A

8. **Country of Citizenship**
- ○ Cambodia
- ○ China
- ○ Colombia
- ○ Dominican Republic
- ○ El Salvador
- ○ Guatemala
- ○ Haiti
- ○ India
- ○ Iran
- ○ Korea
- ○ Laos
- ○ Mexico
- ○ Nicaragua
- ○ Philippines
- ○ Poland
- ○ Russia
- ○ Taiwan
- ○ Vietnam
- ○ Other _____

9. Test Form

9 ☐ ☐ _____

Test Booklet No. _____

10. **Registrant Status**
- ○ Pre-registration
- ○ Walk-in/Late registrant
- ○ Re-take with voucher
- ○ Re-schedule

Writing Test

A.

B.

SAMPLE

Examinee's Signature _____

| For Official Use Only | 1 - 20 ☐ | A ○① ○ PASS |
| | | B ○① ○ FAIL |

Comments

Name _____

Test Site Name _____

PLEASE PRINT YOUR NAME AS IT APPEARS ON YOUR INS CARD

Today's Date _____

PASS ○   FAIL ○

CASAS BASIC CITIZENSHIP SKILLS EXAMINATION - Unofficial Results

Your official notice of test results will be sent to you within three weeks.

ACCU-SCAN™ 69107LS0395 (ReflexRead)
APPERSON BUSINESS FORMS, INC.

010415   010415

Determining the date of eligibility for naturalization from the Resident Alien Card

According to INS regulations, a permanent resident is eligible for naturalization five years after being granted permanent resident status. The time period is only three years from this date if the applicant has been married to a U.S. citizen for those three years.

As shown on the sample cards below, the date of lawful permanent residency status appears on the back of the Resident Alien Card (the "green card"). Cards issued in 1989 or later list the date beginning with the year, then the month, then the day (A). On cards issued before 1989, the date begins with the month, then the day, then the year (B).

Some cards have a TEMP RES ADJ DATE. This is the date the person became a temporary resident. This date should not be used to determine the date of eligibility for naturalization.

Before 1989

front

1989 or later

front

back

(B)

(A) **back**

THE PROCESS
Becoming a naturalized citizen of the United States of America involves a three-step process:

(1) completing and filing an application with the Immigration and Naturalization Service (INS),

(2) being interviewed by an INS official, and

(3) taking an oath of allegiance to the United States.

The application is filed with the INS along with the $95 fee plus the applicant's identification photos, fingerprints, and supporting documents. Applications can be filed directly with the INS through an organization (e.g. the National Association of Latino Elected and Appointed Officials or NALEO) or in person as a "one-stop." One-stop applications are available in certain INS districts for those who have met the English/civics (history and government) requirement and can be interviewed on the day of filing.

THE NINE REQUIREMENTS
There are nine requirements an applicant must meet to become a citizen of the United States of America. An applicant must:

(1) be a lawful permanent resident (A permanent resident is a person who receives an immigrant visa. This visa lawfully admits that person to the United States and allows him or her to work there permanently);

(2) be at least 18 years of age;

(3) have made a home in the United States for at least five years; and

(4) have been physically present in the United States for at least half of the five years preceding the date of application;

(5) not have "disrupted the continuity of one's residence" in the United States for any of the last five years;

(6) be able to speak, read, and write words in ordinary usage in the English language;

(7) be able to pass a civics test (U.S. history and government);

(8) have good moral character, keeping in mind certain bars to naturalization; and

(9) take an oath of loyalty to the United States.

Each of these requirements is explained below.

1. Lawful Permanent Residence
The general rule is that a person must be a lawful permanent resident (LPR) for five years to be eligible to apply for naturalization. However, an applicant can apply for citizenship if she or he has been married to a U.S. citizen (USC) for three years and is not now divorced or legally separated.

The date of adjustment or admission on the Resident Alien Card (I-551 or I-151), or green card, will indicate the beginning of the required five- or three-year period of permanent residence. An Application for Naturalization (N-400) can be filed three months prior to the date of eligibility.

2. Age
An applicant must be at least 18 years old to be naturalized. An applicant can file before age 18 but must be 18 by the date of the interview.

* As of August 1995.

Under certain circumstances U.S.-citizen parents can also apply for citizenship for minor (under 18 years of age) unmarried children. (Minor unmarried children of two U.S.-citizen parents are automatically U.S. citizens.) One U.S.-citizen parent alone can apply for minor unmarried children who are lawful permanent residents (LPR) and who live in the United States. These minor children are not required to meet the English, civics, or residency requirements. If they are under 14 years of age, they do not need to take the oath of naturalization.

3. Residence

An applicant must have resided in the United States for at least five years as a lawful permanent resident or for three years if she or he is the spouse of a U.S. citizen. Residence is defined as "general abode and principal dwelling place." An applicant must live in the state or INS district in which she or he files the petition for at least three months before filing the N-400. An applicant must reside continuously in the United States from the date of application to the time of admission to citizenship.

4. Physical Presence

The applicant must have been physically present in the United States for at least half (30 months) of the five-year residence period discussed above. The spouse of a U.S. citizen needs to have been here for only half of the three-year residence period, or 18 months.

5. Continuity of Residence/Abandonment of Residence

The applicant must not have abandoned her or his residence in the United States. This means that the person must show that she or he has maintained a home in the United States.

If a person has left the United States for more than six months at one time but for less than one year, the INS will deem her or him to have abandoned residence for naturalization unless the person can prove that she or he did not abandon residence. Absences of six months or less will not cause a person to abandon her or his residence. If the applicant left the United States for one year or longer, the INS will automatically deem her or him to have abandoned her or his residence. No one with an absence of more than one year should apply without first consulting with legal counsel.

It is important to note that an applicant **must disclose all absences since becoming a lawful permanent resident**, not just the absences within the last five years.

6. English Language

An applicant must be able to read, write, and speak some English. The naturalization interview is usually conducted in English.

There are three exemptions to the English requirement. Exemptions are made for applicants who <u>on the day of filing:</u>
> (1) are over 50 years old and have lived in the United States for at least 20 years since becoming lawful permanent residents; or
> (2) are over 55 years old and have lived here for at least 15 years since becoming lawful permanent residents; or
> (3) cannot comply with the requirement because of a mental, physical, or developmental disability.

7. United States History and Government

An applicant must understand basic aspects of U.S. civics (history and government). An applicant who fails the U.S. history and government test at an INS interview is given an opportunity to retake the test.

The INS waives the U.S. history and government requirement only for those who on the day of filing are unable to comply with it because of a physical or developmental disability or mental impairment.

The INS makes an allowance for applicants who on the date of filing:
(1) are over 50 years old and have lived in the United States for at least 20 years since becoming lawful permanent residents; or
(2) are over 55 years old and have lived here for at least 15 years since becoming lawful permanent residents.

These two groups will be tested on U.S. history and government in their own language and should bring an interpreter.

Some applicants for naturalization may have fulfilled the U.S. civics requirement as part of the legalization program to become lawful permanent residents through the January 1, 1982, amnesty program.

In order to have fulfilled the U.S. civics requirement for naturalization at the same time she or he fulfilled the legalization requirement for amnesty, the person must have either:
(1) passed a test on English/civics at the INS Phase II interview, also called the "312" test, given by an INS official; or
(2) passed a standardized test on English/civics given by a staff person at certain community agencies. Examples of standardized tests are those provided by the Educational Testing Service (ETS) or the Comprehensive Adult Student Assessment System (CASAS).

A person who fulfilled the amnesty legalization program's English/civics requirement in any other way will need to pass an INS citizenship test to fulfill the citizenship requirement. This applies, for example, to a person who fulfilled the legalization requirement with a U.S. high school diploma or with a Certificate of Satisfactory Pursuit stating that she or he had taken at least 40 hours of an English/civics class.

Special agricultural worker (SAW) applicants did not have to meet the English/civics requirement to obtain permanent resident status, but they have to do so for naturalization.

As of March 24, 1995, the INS gives special consideration to applicants who are over age 65 and who have been living in the United States at least 20 years as lawful permanent residents.* They must correctly answer six of the following ten questions in either their native language or in English:
(1) Who is the president of the United States? (William "Bill" Clinton)
(2) How many states are there in the United States? (50)
(3) What are the colors of the American flag? (Red, white, and blue)
(4) What is the capital of the United States? (Washington, DC)
(5) In what month do we celebrate Independence Day? (July)
(6) Who was the first president of the United States? (George Washington)
(7) What are the three branches of our government? (executive, legislative, and judiciary)
(8) What is the minimum voting age in the United States? (18 years)
(9) Who was the president during the Civil War? (Abraham Lincoln)
(10) What are the first ten amendments to the Constitution called? (The Bill of Rights)

* This practice may change. It is not yet a regulation.

8. Good Moral Character

An applicant for naturalization must have good moral character for the five years immediately before applying for naturalization. The INS does an FBI fingerprint check to discover an applicant's criminal and immigration history. Any police or INS arrests or convictions could affect an applicant's eligibility and possibly jeopardize her or his residency status. Such an applicant should seek legal counsel before completing an application.

9. Belief in Principles of United States and Oath of Allegiance

All applicants for naturalization must demonstrate that they are "attached to the principles of the Constitution of the United States and well disposed to the good order and happiness of the United States." Applicants satisfy this requirement by taking an oath of allegiance when they are sworn in as U.S. citizens at a naturalization ceremony.

OTHER IMPORTANT ISSUES REGARDING ELIGIBILITY FOR CITIZENSHIP
Bars to Naturalization

A person with a deportation order against him or her at the time he or she applies for naturalization cannot become a citizen. If deportation proceedings are stopped, however, he or she can reapply for naturalization.

People who have been involved in certain political activities in the ten years before applying for naturalization are also barred from citizenship. For example, people who have advocated anarchism or totalitarianism cannot be naturalized.

Also barred from citizenship are people who are, or who have been, members of or affiliated with the Communist Party in the ten years before applying for naturalization.

There is an important exception to the ten-year bar. If the person can show that she or he participated in the prohibited activity involuntarily or had to participate to get food, a job, or other necessities, naturalization is not barred.

Permanent Ineligibility to Citizenship

Certain actions, mostly those concerning the military service, can make a person permanently ineligible for U.S. citizenship.

Deserters from the armed forces and draft evaders are permanently ineligible to become U.S. citizens. To be barred from citizenship under this section, however, the person must have been convicted by a court-martial or other court. A person who has applied for and received certain exemptions from U.S. military service based on alien status may be ineligible for citizenship. Failure to register for Selective Service may also be a bar to naturalization. Potential applicants whose experience includes any of these situations should consult an immigration counselor, attorney, or draft counselor.

Selective Service Registration

Since 1980, all men of ages 18 up to and including 25 living in the United States have been required to register with the Selective Service. This requirement includes all men who are U.S. citizens, lawful permanent residents, refugees, asylees, parolees, and undocumented immigrants. The only males between the ages of 18 and 25 not required to register are those who entered the United States as nonimmigrants (e.g. as visitors or students) and who remained in nonimmigrant status until their 26th birthday.

All men required to register must be given the chance to register before naturalization is denied. Men aged 26 and older who should have registered but did not will be denied naturalization, if the failure to register was knowing and willful.

In the past, a person who had failed to register with the Selective Service simply because he never knew that he had to register could write to or call the Selective Service explaining why he had not registered. The Selective Service would then send a letter, known as a Status Information Letter, confirming that the person had not registered with the Selective Service and stating that nothing in their records indicated that the person's failure to register was knowing and willful. If the naturalization applicant's failure to register with the Selective Service became an issue of concern to the INS, the applicant could present his Status Information Letter, along with a statement and/or other evidence, to the INS to prove that his failure to register for the Selective Service was not knowing and willful.

Denied Applications for Naturalization

When denying an application for naturalization, the INS will send the applicant a **written notice** stating the reason for the denial. The applicant can file a request for review with that office within 30 days of the denial. During this review, the applicant can submit any new evidence or testimony to support the application.

If the INS upholds its earlier denial, the applicant can then file for review an appeal with the local federal district court. The applicant must file the appeal within 120 days of the INS final determination. The court must make an entirely new decision on the person's application and must give the person a hearing if she or he wants one.

APPLICATION FOR NATURALIZATION (N-400)

U.S. Department of Justice
Immigration and Naturalization Service

OMB #1115-0009
Application for Naturalization

INSTRUCTIONS

Purpose of This Form.
This form is for use to apply to become a naturalized citizen of the United States.

Who May File.
You may apply for naturalization if:
- you have been a lawful permanent resident for five years;
- you have been a lawful permanent resident for three years, have been married to a United States citizen for those three years, and continue to be married to that U.S. citizen;
- you are the lawful permanent resident child of United States citizen parents; or
- you have qualifying military service.

Children under 18 may automatically become citizens when their parents naturalize. You may inquire at your local Service office for further information. If you do not meet the qualifications listed above but believe that you are eligible for naturalization, you may inquire at your local Service office for additional information.

General Instructions.
Please answer all questions by typing or clearly printing in black ink. Indicate that an item is not applicable with "N/A". If an answer is "none," write "none". If you need extra space to answer any item, attach a sheet of paper with your name and your alien registration number (A#), if any, and indicate the number of the item.

Every application must be properly signed and filed with the correct fee. If you are under 18 years of age, your parent or guardian must sign the application.

If you wish to be called for your examination at the same time as another person who is also applying for naturalization, make your request on a separate cover sheet. Be sure to give the name and alien registration number of that person.

Initial Evidence Requirements.
You must file your application with the following evidence:

A copy of your alien registration card.

Photographs. You must submit two color photographs of yourself taken within 30 days of this application. These photos must be glossy, unretouched and unmounted, and have a white background. Dimension of the face should be about 1 inch from chin to top of hair. Face should be 3/4 frontal view of right side with right ear visible. Using pencil or felt pen, lightly print name and A#, if any, on the back of each photo. This requirement may be waived by the Service if you can establish that you are confined because of age or physical infirmity.

Fingerprints. If you are between the ages of 14 and 75, you must sumit your fingerprints on Form FD-258. Fill out the form and write your Alien Registration Number in the space marked "Your No. OCA" or "Miscellaneous No. MNU". Take the chart and these instructions to a police station, sheriff's office or an office of this Service, or other reputable person or organization for fingerprinting. (You should contact the police or sheriff's office before going there since some of these offices do not take fingerprints for other government agencies.) You must sign the chart in the presence of the person taking your fingerprints and have that person sign his/her name, title, and the date in the space provided. Do not bend, fold, or crease the fingerprint chart.

U.S. Military Service. If you have ever served in the Armed Forces of the United States at any time, you must submit a completed Form G-325B. If your application is based on your military service you must also submit Form N-426, "Request for Certification of Military or Naval Service."

Application for Child. If this application is for a permanent resident child of U.S. citizen parents, you must also submit copies of the child's birth certificate, the parents' marriage certificate, and evidence of the parents' U.S. citizenship. If the parents are divorced, you must also submit the divorce decree and evidence that the citizen parent has legal custody of the child.

Where to File.
File this application at the local Service office having jurisdiction over your place of residence.

Fee.
The fee for this application is $90.00. The fee must be submitted in the exact amount. It cannot be refunded. DO NOT MAIL CASH.

All checks and money orders must be drawn on a bank or other institution located in the United States and must be payable in United States currency. The check or money order should be made payable to the Immigration and Naturalization Service, except that:
- If you live in Guam, and are filing this application in Guam, make your check or money order payable to the "Treasurer, Guam."
- If you live in the Virgin Islands, and are filing this application in the Virgin Islands, make your check or money order payable to the "Commissioner of Finance of the Virgin Islands."

Checks are accepted subject to collection. An uncollected check will render the application and any document issued invalid. A charge of $5.00 will be imposed if a check in payment of a fee is not honored by the bank on which it is drawn.

Processing Information.

Rejection. Any application that is not signed or is not accompanied by the proper fee will be rejected with a notice that the application is deficient. You may correct the deficiency and resubmit the application. However, an application is not considered properly filed until it is accepted by the Service.

Requests for more information. We may request more information or evidence. We may also request that you submit the originals of any copy. We will return these originals when they are no longer required.

Interview. After you file your application, you will be notified to appear at a Service office to be examined under oath or affirmation. This interview may not be waived. If you are an adult, you must show that you have a knowledge and understanding of the history, principles, and form of government of the United States. There is no exemption from this requirement.

You will also be examined on your ability to read, write, and speak English. If on the date of your examination you are more than 50 years of age and have been a lawful permanent resident for 20 years or more, or you are 55 years of age and have been a lawful permanent resident for at least 15 years, you will be exempt from the English language requirements of the law. If you are exempt, you may take the examination in any language you wish.

Oath of Allegiance. If your application is approved, you will be required to take the following oath of allegiance to the United States in order to become a citizen:

"I hereby declare, on oath, that I absolutely and entirely renounce and abjure all allegiance and fidelity to any foreign prince, potentate, state or sovereignty, of whom or which I have heretofore been a subject or citizen; that I will support and defend the Constitution and laws of the United States of America against all enemies, foreign and domestic; that I will bear true faith and allegiance to the same; that I will bear arms on behalf of the United States when required by the law; that I will perform noncombatant service in the armed forces of the United States when required by the law; that I will perform work of national importance under civilian direction when required by the law; and that I take this obligation freely without any mental reservation or purpose of evasion; so help me God."

If you cannot promise to bear arms or perform noncombatant service because of religious training and belief, you may omit those statements when taking the oath. "Religious training and belief" means a person's belief in relation to a Supreme Being involving duties superior to those arising from any human relation, but does not include essentially political, sociological, or philosophical views or merely a personal moral code.

Oath ceremony. You may choose to have the oath of allegiance administered in a ceremony conducted by the Service or request to be scheduled for an oath ceremony in a court that has jurisdiction over the applicant's place of residence. At the time of your examination you will be asked to elect either form of ceremony. You will become a citizen on the date of the oath ceremony and the Attorney General will issue a Certificate of Naturalization as evidence of United States citizenship.

If you wish to change your name as part of the naturalization process, you will have to take the oath in court.

Penalties.

If you knowingly and willfully falsify or conceal a material fact or submit a false document with this request, we will deny the benefit you are filing for, and may deny any other immigration benefit. In addition, you will face severe penalties provided by law, and may be subject to criminal prosecution.

Privacy Act Notice.

We ask for the information on this form, and associated evidence, to determine if you have established eligibility for the immigration benefit you are filing for. Our legal right to ask for this information is in 8 USC 1439, 1440, 1443, 1445, 1446, and 1452. We may provide this information to other government agencies. Failure to provide this information, and any requested evidence, may delay a final decision or result in denial of your request.

Paperwork Reduction Act Notice.

We try to create forms and instructions that are accurate, can be easily understood, and which impose the least possible burden on you to provide us with information. Often this is difficult because some immigration laws are very complex. Accordingly, the reporting burden for this collection of information is computed as follows: (1) learning about the law and form, 20 minutes; (2) completing the form, 25 minutes; and (3) assembling and filing the application (includes statutory required interview and travel time, after filing of application), 3 hours and 35 minutes, for an estimated average of 4 hours and 20 minutes per response. If you have comments regarding the accuracy of this estimate, or suggestions for making this form simpler, you can write to both the Immigration and Naturalization Service, 425 I Street, N.W., Room 5304, Washington, D.C. 20536; and the Office of Management and Budget, Paperwork Reduction Project, OMB No. 1115-0009, Washington, D.C. 20503.

START HERE - Please Type or Print

Part 1. Information about you.

Family Name	Given Name	Middle Initial

U.S. Mailing Address - Care of

Street Number and Name		Apt. #
City	County	
State	ZIP Code	

Date of Birth (month/day/year)	Country of Birth
Social Security #	A #

Part 2. Basis for Eligibility (check one).

a. ☐ I have been a permanent resident for at least five (5) years .

b. ☐ I have been a permanent resident for at least three (3) years and have been married to a United States Citizen for those three years.

c. ☐ I am a permanent resident child of United States citizen parent(s) .

d. ☐ I am applying on the basis of qualifying military service in the Armed Forces of the U.S. and have attached completed Forms N-426 and G-325B

e. ☐ Other. (Please specify section of law) _____ .

Part 3. Additional information about you.

Date you became a permanent resident (month/day/year)	Port admitted with an immmigrant visa or INS Office where granted adjustment of status.

Citizenship

Name on alien registration card (if different than in Part 1)

Other names used since you became a permanent resident (including maiden name)

Sex ☐ Male ☐ Female	Height	Marital Status: ☐ Single ☐ Married	☐ Divorced ☐ Widowed

Can you speak, read and write English ?   ☐No ☐Yes.

Absences from the U.S.:

Have you been absent from the U.S. since becoming a permanent resident?   ☐ No ☐Yes.

If you answered **"Yes"** , complete the following, Begin with your most recent absence. If you need more room to explain the reason for an absence or to list more trips, continue on separate paper.

Date left U.S.	Date returned	Did absence last 6 months or more?	Destination	Reason for trip
		☐ Yes ☐ No		
		☐ Yes ☐ No		
		☐ Yes ☐ No		
		☐ Yes ☐ No		
		☐ Yes ☐ No		
		☐ Yes ☐ No		

Form N-400 (Rev. 07/17/91)N   **Continued on back.**

FOR INS USE ONLY

Returned	Receipt
Resubmitted	
Reloc Sent	
Reloc Rec'd	
☐ Applicant Interviewed	

At interview
☐ request naturalization ceremony at court

Remarks

Action

To Be Completed by
Attorney or *Representative*, if any
☐ Fill in box if G-28 is attached to represent the applicant

VOLAG#

ATTY State License #

Part 4. Information about your residences and employment.

A. List your addresses during the last five (5) years or since you became a permanent resident, whichever is less. Begin with your current address. If you need more space, continue on separate paper:

Street Number and Name, City, State, Country, and Zip Code	Dates (month/day/year)	
	From	To

B. List your employers during the last five (5) years. List your present or most recent employer first. If none, write "None". If you need more space, continue on separate paper.

Employer's Name	Employer's Address		Dates Employed (month/day/year)		Occupation/position
	Street Name and Number - City, State and ZIP Code		From	To	

Part 5. Information about your marital history.

A. Total number of times you have been married _____ . If you are now married, complete the following regarding your husband or wife.

Family name	Given name	Middle initial

Address

Date of birth (month/day/year)	Country of birth	Citizenship
Social Security#	A# (if applicable)	Immigration status (If not a U.S. citizen)

Naturalization (If applicable)
(month/day/year)   Place   (City, State)

If you have ever previously been married or if your current spouse has been previously married, please provide the following on separate paper: Name of prior spouse, date of marriage, date marriage ended, how marriage ended and immigration status of prior spouse.

Part 6. Information about your children.

B. Total Number of Children _____ Complete the following information for each of your children. If the child lives with you, state "with me" in the address column; otherwise give city/state/country of child's current residence. If deceased, write "deceased" in the address column. If you need more space, continue on separate paper.

Full name of child	Date of birth	Country of birth	Citizenship	A - Number	Address

Form N-400 (Rev 07/17/91)N   *Continued on next page*

Part 7. Additional eligibility factors.

Please answer each of the following questions. If your answer is **"Yes"**, explain on a separate paper.

1. Are you now, or have you ever been a member of, or in any way connected or associated with the Communist Party, or ever knowingly aided or supported the Communist Party directly, or indirectly through another organization, group or person, or ever advocated, taught, believed in, or knowingly supported or furthered the interests of communism?   ☐ Yes   ☐ No

2. During the period March 23, 1933 to May 8, 1945, did you serve in, or were you in any way affiliated with, either directly or indirectly, any military unit, paramilitary unit, police unit, self-defense unit, vigilante unit, citizen unit of the Nazi party or SS, government agency or office, extermination camp, concentration camp, prisoner of war camp, prison, labor camp, detention camp or transit camp, under the control or affiliated with:

    a. The Nazi Government of Germany?   ☐ Yes   ☐ No

    b. Any government in any area occupied by, allied with, or established with the assistance or cooperation of, the Nazi Government of Germany?   ☐ Yes   ☐ No

3. Have you at any time, anywhere, ever ordered, incited, assisted, or otherwise participated in the persecution of any person because of race, religion, national origin, or political opinion?   ☐ Yes   ☐ No

4. Have you ever left the United States to avoid being drafted into the U.S. Armed Forces?   ☐ Yes   ☐ No

5. Have you ever failed to comply with Selective Service laws?   ☐ Yes   ☐ No
    If you have registered under the Selective Service laws, complete the following information:
    Selective Service Number:_____ Date Registered:_____
    If you registered before 1978, also provide the following:
    Local Board Number:_____ Classification:_____

6. Did you ever apply for exemption from military service because of alienage, conscientious objections or other reasons?   ☐ Yes   ☐ No

7. Have you ever deserted from the military, air or naval forces of the United States?   ☐ Yes   ☐ No

8. Since becoming a permanent resident , have you ever failed to file a federal income tax return ?   ☐ Yes   ☐ No

9. Since becoming a permanent resident , have you filed a federal income tax return as a nonresident or failed to file a federal return because you considered yourself to be a nonresident?   ☐ Yes   ☐ No

10 Are deportation proceedings pending against you, or have you ever been deported, or ordered deported, or have you ever applied for suspension of deportation?   ☐ Yes   ☐ No

11. Have you ever claimed in writing, or in any way, to be a United States citizen?   ☐ Yes   ☐ No

12. Have you ever:

    a. been a habitual drunkard?   ☐ Yes   ☐ No

    b. advocated or practiced polygamy?   ☐ Yes   ☐ No

    c. been a prostitute or procured anyone for prostitution?   ☐ Yes   ☐ No

    d. knowingly and for gain helped any alien to enter the U.S. illegally?   ☐ Yes   ☐ No

    e. been an illicit trafficker in narcotic drugs or marijuana?   ☐ Yes   ☐ No

    f. received income from illegal gambling?   ☐ Yes   ☐ No

    g. given false testimony for the purpose of obtaining any immigration benefit?   ☐ Yes   ☐ No

13. Have you ever been declared legally incompetent or have you ever been confined as a patient in a mental institution?   ☐ Yes   ☐ No

14. Were you born with, or have you acquired in same way, any title or order of nobility in any foreign State?   ☐ Yes   ☐ No

15. Have you ever:

    a. knowingly committed any crime for which you have not been arrested?   ☐ Yes   ☐ No

    b. been arrested, cited, charged, indicted, convicted, fined or imprisoned for breaking or violating any law or ordinance excluding traffic regulations?   ☐ Yes   ☐ No

(If you answer yes to 15 , in your explanation give the following information for each incident or occurrence the **city**, **state**, and **country**, where the offense took place, the **date** and **nature** of the offense, and the **outcome** or **disposition** of the case).

Part 8. Allegiance to the U.S.

If your answer to any of the following questions is **"NO"**, attach a full explanation:

1. Do you believe in the Constitution and form of government of the U.S.?   ☐ Yes   ☐ No

2. Are you willing to take the full Oath of Allegiance to the U.S.? (see instructions)   ☐ Yes   ☐ No

3. If the law requires it, are you willing to bear arms on behalf of the U.S.?   ☐ Yes   ☐ No

4. If the law requires it, are you willing to perform noncombatant services in the Armed Forces of the U.S.?   ☐ Yes   ☐ No

5. If the law requires it, are you willing to perform work of national importance under civilian direction?   ☐ Yes   ☐ No

Part 9. Memberships and organizations.

A. List your present and past membership in or affiliation with every organization, association, fund, foundation, party, club, society, or similar group in the United States or in any other place. Include any military service in this part. If none, write "none". Include the name of organization, location, dates of membership and the nature of the organization. If additional space is needed, use separate paper.

Part 10. Complete only if you checked block " C " in Part 2.

How many of your parents are U.S. citizens?   ☐ One   ☐ Both   (Give the following about one U.S. citizen parent:)

Family Name	Given Name	Middle Name
Address		

Basis for citizenship:
☐ Birth
☐ Naturalization Cert. No.

Relationship to you (check one):   ☐ natural parent   ☐ adoptive parent

☐ parent of child legitimated after birth

If adopted or legitimated after birth, give date of adoption or, legitimation: *(month/day/year)* _____

Does this parent have legal custody of you?   ☐ Yes   ☐ No

(Attach a copy of relating evidence to establish that you are the child of this U.S. citizen and evidence of this parent's citizenship.)

Part 11. Signature. *(Read the information on penalties in the instructions before completing this section).*

I certify or, if outside the United States, I swear or affirm, under penalty of perjury under the laws of the United States of America that this application, and the evidence submitted with it, is all true and correct. I authorize the release of any information from my records which the Immigration and Naturalization Service needs to determine eligibility for the benefit I am seeking.

Signature _____   Date _____

Please Note: If you do not completely fill out this form, or fail to submit required documents listed in the instructions, you may not be found eligible for naturalization and this application may be denied.

Part 12. Signature of person preparing form if other than above. *(Sign below)*

I declare that I prepared this application at the request of the above person and it is based on all information of which I have knowledge.

Signature _____   **Print Your Name** _____   Date _____

Firm Name and Address _____

DO NOT COMPLETE THE FOLLOWING UNTIL INSTRUCTED TO DO SO AT THE INTERVIEW

I swear that I know the contents of this application, and supplemental pages 1 through_____, that the corrections , numbered 1 through_____, were made at my request, and that this amended application, is true to the best of my knowledge and belief.

_____
(Complete and true signature of applicant)

Subscribed and sworn to before me by the applicant.

_____
(Examiner's Signature)   Date

NOTICE OF NATURALIZATION OATH CEREMONY

U.S. Department of Justice
Immigration and Naturalization Service

OMB No. 1115-0052
Notice of Naturalization Oath Ceremony

AR # _____

Date _____

●   ●

●   ●

___   ___

You are hereby notified to appear for a Naturalization Oath Ceremony on:

at: DIRKSEN FEDERAL BUILDING   (CEREMONIAL COURT   )
        219 SOUTH DEARBORN STREET   25TH FLOOR
        CHICAGO, ILLINOIS 60604   ROOM 2525

Please report promptly at _____ 7:45 A. **M**.

NOTE*   MEN SHOULD WEAR SUIT JACKET AND TIE.
        ABSOLUTELY NO <u>SHORTS</u>, <u>JEANS</u> OR <u>TENNIS SHOES</u>

        PLEASE LIMIT <u>GUESTS</u> TO <u>ONE</u> FOR <u>EACH NEW CITIZEN</u>

        <u>PROPER</u> ATTIRE IS <u>REQUIRED</u>

You must being the following with you:

☒ This letter, WITH ALL OF THE QUESTIONS ON THE OTHER SIDE ANSWERED IN INK OR ON A TYPEWRITER.
☒ Alien Registration Card.
☒ Reentry Permit, or Refugee Travel Document.
☒ Any Immigration documents you may have.
☒ If the naturalization application is on behalf of your child (children), bring your child (children).
☐ Other

Proper attire should be worn.

If you cannot come to this ceremony, return this notice immediately and state why you cannot appear. In such case, you will be sent another notice of ceremony at a later date. You must appear at an oath ceremony to complete the naturalization process.

Form N-445 (Rev. 1/8/92)   **(SEE OTHER SIDE)**

In connection with your application for naturalization, please answer each of the questions by checking "Yes" or "No". You should answer these questions the day you are to appear for the citizenship oath ceremony. These questions refer to actions since the date you were first interviewed on your <u>Application for Naturalization</u>. They do not refer to anything that happened before that interview.

After you have answered every question, sign your name and fill in the date and place of signing, and provide your current address.

You must bring this completed questionnaire with you to the oath ceremony, as well as the documents indicated on the front, and give them to the Immigration employee at the oath ceremony. You may be questioned further on your answers at that time.

AFTER the date you were first interviewed on your Application for Naturaliztion, Form N-400:

ANSWERS

1. Have you married, or been widowed, separated, or divorced? (If "Yes" please bring documented proof of marriage, death, separation or divorce.)

    1. ☐ Yes ☐ No

2. Have you traveled outside the United States?

    2. ☐ Yes ☐ No

3. Have you knowingly committed any crime or offense, for which you have not been arrested; or have you been arrested, cited, charged, indicted, convicted, fined, or imprisoned for breaking or violating any law or ordinance, including traffic violations?

    3. ☐ Yes ☐ No

4. Have you joined any organization, including the Communist Party, or become associated or connected therewith in any way?

    4. ☐ Yes ☐ No

5. Have you claimed exemption from military service?

    5. ☐ Yes ☐ No

6. Has there been any change in your willingness to bear arms on behalf of the United States; to perform non-combatant service in the armed forces of the United States; to perform work of national importance under civilian direction, if the law requires it?

    6. ☐ Yes ☐ No

7. Have you practiced polygamy; received income from illegal gambling; been a prostitute, procured anyone for prostitution or been involved in any other unlawful commercialized vice; encouraged or helped any alien to enter the United States illegally; illicitly trafficked in drugs or marihuana; given any false testimony to obtain immigration benefits; or been a habitual drunkard?

    7. ☐ Yes ☐ No

I certify that each of the answers shown above were made by me or at my direction, and that they are true and correct.

Signed at _____ , on _____

(City and State)   (Date)

_____   _____

(Full Signature)   (Full Address and ZIP Code)

Authority for collection of the information requested on Form N-445 is contained in Sections 101(f), 316, 332, 335 and 336 of the Immigration and Nationality Act (8 U.S.C. 1101 (f), 1427, 1443, 1446 and 1447). Submission of the information is voluntary. The principal purposes for requesting the information are to enable examiners of the Immigration and Naturalization Service to determine an applicant's eligibility for naturalization. The information requested may, as a matter of routine use, be disclosed to naturalization courts and to other federal, state, local or foreign law enforcement and regulatory agencies, the Department of Defense, including any component thereof, the Selective Service System, the Department of State, the Department of the Treasury, the Department of Transportation, Central Intelligence Agency, Interpol and individuals and organizations in the processing of any application for naturalization, or during the course of investigation to elicit further information required by the Immigration and Naturalization Service to carry out its functions. Information solicited which indicates a violation or potential violation of law, whether civil, criminal, or regulatory in nature, may be referred, as a routine use, to the appropriate agency, whether federal, state, local or foreign, charged with the responsibility of investigating, enforcing or prosecuting such violations. Failure to provide all or any of the requested information may result in a denial of the application for naturalization.

Public Reporting burden for this collection of information is estimated to average 5 minutes per response, including the time for reviewing instructions, searching existing data sources, gathering and maintaining the data needed, and completing and reviewing the collection of information. Send comments regarding this burden estimate or any other aspect of this collection of information, including suggestions for reducing this burden to: U.S. Department of Justice, Immigration and Naturalization Service, (Room 5304), Washington, DC 20536; and to the Office of Management and Budget, Paperwork Reduction Project: OMB No. 1115-0052,; Washington, DC 20503.

*U.S. GPO: 1992-312-328/51138

CERTIFICATE OF NATURALIZATION

NO. A0 000 000

INS Registration No.

I certify that the description given is true, and that the photograph affixed hereto is a likeness of me.

_____
(Complete and true signature of holder)

Personal description of holder as of date of naturalization:

Date of Birth:

Sex:

Height: _____ feet _____ inches

Marital Status:

Country of former nationality:

Be it known that, pursuant to an application filed with the Attorney General

at:

The Attorney General having found that:

SPECIMEN

than residing in the United States, intends to reside in the United States when so required by the Naturalization Laws of the United States, and had in all other respects complied with the applicable provisions of such naturalization laws and was entitled to be admitted to citizenship, such person having taken the oath of allegiance in a ceremony conducted by the

at:

on:

that such person is admitted as citizen of the United States of America.

_____
Commissioner of Immigration and Naturalization

(SECURELY AND PERMANENTLY AFFIX PHOTOGRAPH HERE)

(A SEAL WILL BE IMPRESSED SO AS TO COVER A PORTION OF THE LOWER EDGE OF THE PHOTOGRAPH)

IT IS PUNISHABLE BY U.S. LAW TO COPY, PRINT OR PHOTOGRAPH THIS CERTIFICATE, WITHOUT LAWFUL AUTHORITY.